CHILD
an overview
PROTECTION
of child abuse
POLICY
issues and practice in
PRACTICE
social work departments
AND
in Scotland
PROCEDURE

EDINBURGH: HMSO

First published 1992

PREFACE

In an effort to assist the Orkney Inquiry the Directors of Social Work in Scotland have sought to compile an overview of social work practice in the field of child abuse and child protection services across Scotland.

This overview of child abuse issues and practice which face social workers and the local authority departments which employ them has been completed with the valued assistance of staff who have key roles as managers, social workers and trainers in the field of child protection services.

Directors of Social Work and their senior colleagues are concerned that events which have taken place in Orkney should be considered within a general framework of seeking to understand the issues and practice common to Scottish authorities.

Tayside	Shetland	Fife
Peter J Bates	Bill Bennett	Allan Bowman
Borders	**Lothian**	**Highland**
Sandy Cameron	John Chant	James Dick
Strathclyde	**Grampian**	**Western Isles**
Fred E Edwards	Mary C Hartnoll	Norma E MacLeod
Central	**Dumfries and Galloway**	
Ian Ross	Faith Simpson	

Footnote: Mr Paul Lee, the Director of Social Work in Orkney, could not participate in the preparation of this report because of his direct involvement in the Inquiry.

ACKNOWLEDGEMENTS

Directors of Social Work in Scotland are grateful for the work undertaken in preparing this overview of issues and practice in the field of child abuse to the following:

Mr James Airth, Principal Officer, Highland Regional Council

Mr John Chant, Director of Social Work, Lothian Regional Council

Mr Peter David, Principal Social Worker, Dumfries & Galloway Regional Council

Ms Harriet Dempster, Principal Officer (Child Protection), Tayside Regional Council

Ms Bernadette Docherty, District Officer (Child Care), Strathclyde Regional Council

Mr Colin Findlay, Principal Officer (Child Protection), Central Regional Council

Mr Keith Harper, Senior Social Worker, Borders Regional Council

Mr Sandy Jamieson, former Assistant Director of Social Work, Strathclyde Regional Council

Mr Iain MacAulay, Area Social Work Manager, Western Isles Islands Council

Mr John McBride, Senior Principal Social Worker, Lothian Regional Council

Ms Jacquie Roberts, Project Head, Polepark Family Counselling Centre, Tayside Regional Council

Dr Sue Ross, Assistant Director of Social Work, Borders Regional Council

Mr Gordon Sinclair, Senior Social Worker, Grampian Regional Council

Mr Raymond Taylor, Training Officer (Child Care), Central Regional Council

Mr Ron Taylor, Principal Officer, Highland Regional Council

Mr Peter Tempest, Assistant Director of Social Work, Fife Regional Council

Special thanks are due to:
Mr David Gough, Senior Research Fellow, Public Health Research Unit, University of Glasgow, who completed a significant piece of research for us in a relatively short period of time and,
Ms Jane Murray, Administrative Secretary, Lothian Regional Council Department of Social Work who patiently brought together our many manuscripts and gave invaluable assistance in the typing and presentation of our report, and together with
Ms Pat Gaudin, Business and Communications Manager, Lothian Regional Council Department of Social Work undertook final editorial and production work.

ISSUES

- **Children experience many and varied forms of abuse.**
- **There is a need for a more structured approach to learning and training.**
- **Sexual abuse can and does include adults acting in concert to exploit a child or children for sexual gratification.**
- **There is a continuing requirement to establish definitions that are widely accepted and consistently applied.**
- **The linking of child sexual abuse with ceremonial and ritualistic behaviour has provoked powerful emotions and responses. In a professional context, the issue is not one of belief or non-belief. It is the assessment of what has happened to children and the gathering of systematic evidence to aid the establishment of a sound knowledge base.**
- **Social workers are frequently required to work at the boundaries of the existing knowledge base. In such circumstances, work must be guided by basic values and established principles.**
- **There is a high degree of commonality in the values and principles which inform social work practice in Scotland.**
- **The assessment of complex cases involving child sex abuse can be a difficult task for most experienced practitioners. Professional judgements must be influenced by the interests of the child, the requirements of law and the knowledge that the child might continue to be abused.**
- **The experience of practitioners should be drawn together to allow the formulation of guidance to practitioners in dealing with cases in which more than one adult is believed to be involved.**
- **Social Work as a profession needs to establish reliable arrangements to test and disseminate new knowledge.**
- **Intervention must not be led by considerations relating to the collection of evidence.**
- **Throughout any investigation, evaluation or intervention, the interests and needs of the child victim should predominate and the process should secure that end. The wider interests of the community are an important consideration that should not be pursued at the risk of further harm to the child who has been the victim.**
- **It is for each social work authority to adopt arrangements for the deployment of skilled staff which are best suited to the needs of the community it serves.**
- **The practice of involving parents in case conferences varies widely across Scotland. Further advice and guidance for all agencies involved should be formulated to achieve greater consistency of practice.**
- **There is an urgent need to direct increased resources to local authorities to ensure consistent standards of training.**
- **The length for qualifying training courses for social workers should be extended from two years to three years.**
- **There is an urgent need for joint training opportunities for staff from Police, Social Work, Health, Education and Voluntary Organisations.**
- **Training on child care and child protection issues to a specified standard should be provided for Children's Panel members and Sheriffs.**

- Joint work between Police and Social Work in relation to child sexual abuse requires further development to achieve consistent practice.
- Problems will not be resolved by routine undifferentiated joint action or by unco-ordinated autonomous action.
- Directors of Social Work strongly support the framework of Scottish Child Care Law and the Children's Hearing System.
- Perceptions and definitions of children's needs change, as do society's perceptions of the rights and responsibilities of the state, parents and children.
- Developments in child protection practice have had major implications for the Children's Hearing System.
- The extent to which Reporters exercise discretion in their role varies across Scotland. Discretion should be set within an overall framework and arrangements introduced to ensure a sufficient measure of accountability to standardise practice.
- To command public confidence in complex cases involving compulsory measures of care, it is essential that the children's hearing system is regarded as being fair by parents and children.
- The impartiality and independence of Hearings may require underpinning by measures designed to increase the opportunity for, and ability of, parents and children to participate in proceedings on a basis of greater equality.
- Further consideration should be given to strengthen the role and availability of safeguarders in contentious cases.
- Rules and procedures which frame the Children's Hearing System should be reviewed. Decisions should take account of the increased number of child abuse referrals, the practice guidance which has been directed at Social Work Departments and other key agencies such as Health, Education and Police. These findings, together with a shift in public attitudes, require a more explicit balance to be demonstrated between the paramountcy of the interests of children and a respect for, and representation of, the interests of parents.
- In situations where the effect of the Hearing's decision is to deprive parents of their rights or children of their liberty, change should be introduced to allow the interests of children and parents to be separately represented. Given such serious considerations, Directors would argue that only experienced Panel members who have completed advanced training to a specified standard should be involved in dealing with abuse cases and cases potentially involving a loss of liberty for the child. The rules framing the Hearing itself should be amended to allow independent scrutiny of proposals by safeguarders in contentious cases where rights are in question, and separate representation of the interests of children and parents.
- Directors of Social Work take the view that rules governing Hearings should be altered to allow the Chairperson of the Hearing to meet with the child or young person to hear their views and to agree with the child or young person how the content of their discussion is to be communicated to the other parties involved. In this context consideration should be given to the gender of the Chairperson.
- When access has been terminated and such a decision or recommendation confirmed by a Children's Hearing, it is the view of Directors that parents should have a right of appeal to a Sheriff Court where their interests and that of the child can be formally represented.

CONTENTS

PART I: EVOLVING KNOWLEDGE

PART II: VALUES AND PRINCIPLES

PART III: SOCIAL WORK PRACTICE

PART IV: TRAINING

PART V: INTER-AGENCY COLLABORATION

PART VI: SOCIAL WORK AND THE CHILDREN'S HEARING SYSTEM

PART VII: SOCIAL WORK IN ISLANDS AUTHORITIES AND SPARSELY POPULATED AREAS

PART VIII: THE ROLE OF THE DIRECTOR AND SENIOR STAFF

PART IX: SURVEY OF CHILD PROTECTION REGISTERS 1990-1991 (D.A. GOUGH)

PART I

EVOLVING KNOWLEDGE

1.1.0 HISTORICAL PERSPECTIVE

1.1.1 An examination of history provides ample evidence that children have been exploited and abused physically and sexually down the centuries (Gordon, 1988, Clark, 1987, Parton, 1985).

1.1.2 The universal acceptance of the paramountcy of the blood tie, the very special nature of the parent-child relationship as a cornerstone of society, the family's right to privacy and, until recently, the notion that children are the property of their parents has served to mask the suffering of some children and keep problems hidden.

1.1.3 Since Henry Kempe "discovered" the battered baby syndrome and published his seminal paper on the subject in 1962 there has been a spate of research papers and publications on the subject of child abuse (Kempe, 1962, Kalisch 1978). Academic and professional interest has been parallelled in the media. The issue is regularly in the headlines and constantly achieves high profile status. The protection of children from abuse ranks as the top priority in social work.

1.1.4 In the UK, child abuse has been recognised as a major social problem within the past twenty years. The inquiry into the death of Maria Colwell heralded the recognition of child abuse as a social phenomenon and directed public and professional attention to the practice of social work, the effectiveness of the legal framework and the responsibilities of local authority social work departments.

1.1.5 The "battered child syndrome", essentially a medical definition of a pattern of social behaviour, has evolved through non-accidental injury to the more broadly prescribed term Child Abuse which encompasses not only physical abuse, neglect, failure to thrive and emotional abuse, but the abuse of children for sexual purposes by individuals acting alone or in groups.

1.1.6 Recognition of ways in which children are abused has depended on the willingness of adults, particularly professionals, to look beyond initial presentation of a child's hurt, to hear and listen to what children have to say, to elucidate and inquire into the context of the child's account, to evaluate the information established and exercise a careful professional judgement with the child's interests being given paramount consideration.

1.1.7 The transformation and expansion of the concept of abuse has been rapid and very recent. This is clearly illustrated in a review of Government guidance on child abuse relating to England and Wales. In 1974 reference is made to the fact that older children may be at risk of physical injury. By 1980 the risks of neglect, failure to thrive and emotional abuse are mentioned. The existence of sexual abuse is not acknowledged until 1986.

1.1.8 *In summary, child abuse is not a new problem; what is new is the heightened public awareness. This increased sensitivity has resulted in not only greater numbers of children coming to the attention of Social Work Departments, but also a recognition that children experience many and varied forms of abuse.*

1.2.0 THE COMMUNITY'S RESPONSE

1.2.1 Changes in the rate of recognition of child abuse have not occurred within a static context. Views about the nature and extent of intervention into family life have undergone considerable shifts. However, these shifts have not been uniform nor in a single direction. Public and political attitudes appear to professional workers to vacillate, unable to strike a consistent balance between the interests of children and the rights of parents in a manner which can be framed in law or underpin professional practice.

1.2.2 Against this background of uncertain public attitude various pressure groups have emerged. The profile of abused children has been raised in the context of fund-raising activities by reputable voluntary organisations as well as by the activities of evangelical groups concerned to promote the recognition of children being abused in the context of ceremonial or ritualised activities. *Within Social Work and other professions, interest groups have sought to promulgate experience and theory, some of which has been untested in any disciplined way. What is needed is a more structured approach to validated training and learning.*

1.2.3 Various inquiries into the deaths of Jasmine Beckford (London Borough of Brent 1985), Kimberley Carlile (London Borough of Greenwich in 1986) and Tyra Hendry (London Borough of Lambeth 1987) advocated that social work should take up a much more interventionist stance in its work with families. The importance of using the legislation to protect children was emphasised.

1.2.4 A reaction to the numerous inquiries into the circumstances in which children, often identified as at risk, have died as a result of injuries sustained in physical abuse has been a shift from talking about child abuse and a move towards referring to child protection. This has been viewed as the agencies taking on a more positive approach and preventive role, but it also involves the net being cast more widely. The social work task is to assess not only whether a child has been abused, but whether a child is at risk of abuse. The concepts of "dangerousness and dangerous families" have emerged as part of this child protection movement. Implicit in such arrangements is a statement of attitude about the role of social workers toward the child and its family which may set their approach before they engage in contact with the family.

1.2.5 The admission to care of a significant number of children on place of safety orders in Cleveland in 1987 gave rise to public concern about the way in which the various authorities co-ordinated their work in cases of alleged child sex abuse and used statutory powers to intervene with families. The subsequent inquiry and report highlighted that child sex abuse was a real and serious problem; that children's needs and interests should be pre-eminent; that they are people not objects of concern; that parents should be involved and engaged in the process of assessment; that close working relationships between Health, Social Work and Police were of critical importance to careful assessment and sensitive intervention; that training and support are necessary to assist staff to undertake work in this field; that new research was needed to secure the knowledge base.

The impact of the Cleveland Inquiry led professionals to a more cautious approach to intervention. In Scotland the implications were more muted, the problem was seen to be related to the English legal mechanisms rather than essentially related to the knowledge base and inter-agency practice.

1.3.0 THE EMOTIONAL IMPACT

1.3.1 Child abuse must also be understood within the context of the strong emotions that the subject provokes. This is particularly so in relation to people's ability to face, and to accept, the occurrence of young children being abused for sexual gratification by adults acting alone or in groups. The strength of the emotional responses, and the ability to accept that abuse has taken place, can influence policy and be influenced by an individual's own experience (Wyatt 1988, Fox Harding 1991). Survivors may find the subject much more painful to deal with, they may prove more able to accept the reality and meaning of the abuse than individuals who cannot conceive of the horrors involved.

1.3.2 The emotional block that some people experience may be particularly relevant in trying to approach the issue of adults acting with others in an organised group or a network of contacts for the purpose of seeking sexual gratification through the abuse of young children. The public has not felt comfortable with the identification of widespread sexual abuse. Powerful emotions can surge up in response to child abuse, ranging from anger, moral outrage, hysteria and disgust to downright denial and disbelief. For most people the reality of child abuse is totally at odds with the parental instinct to care for one's child. One way of reconciling this has been to push the problem away and adopt a "them and us" ideology. It is much easier to think about people who abuse children as sick/perverted. This may allow recognition of the problem as a product of individual psychopathology, but may also act as an inhibitor to accepting the scale of abuse as experienced by children.

1.4.0 THEORETICAL PERSPECTIVES

1.4.1 In the post-war period, the medical profession has had a primary role in contributing to a definition of child abuse. The choice of the term, Battered Baby Syndrome, was no accident and served to liken the issue to a disease which could be treated (Kempe 1962). Individual psychopathology was identified as a root cause of the problem. A similar analysis was adopted by psychiatry to explain sexual abuse. Sexual abuse, it was argued, was the product of dysfunctional families (Bentovim, 1987).

1.4.2 However, the inadequacy of the medical model has been clearly established. Research studies have failed to isolate any consistent predictive factors in individuals or families which make them more at risk of abuse. A number of writers have highlighted the flaws in the family systems view of sexual abuse (McLeod and Saraga, 1988; Will, 1988).

1.4.3 It is now clear that in order to understand child abuse, it is necessary to go beyond an examination of individual or family factors. The problem must be set within a social context. The impact of race, gender and class needs to be taken into account in the analysis. Sexual abuse is unlikely to be attributed to a single factor and, therefore, needs to be set in social, situational and individual dimensions to develop a framework of understanding.

1.4.4 The emergence and emphases of the Children's Rights Movement serve to provide a better balance between the rights of children and the responsibilities of parents. Directors of Social Work, together with their senior colleagues, endorse the United Nations Convention on the Rights of the Child which states that all children should have the right to provision, protection and participation and be allowed to grow up free from all forms of exploitation.

It defines exploitation or abuse as any act of commission or omission which results in harm to a child or which results in a child not reaching his/her potential. Framed in this way, child abuse is not just about how parents or carers behave towards children, but also how children are treated and fare via the actions or inactions of the state in developing social policies related to the welfare of children.

1.4.5 The children's rights perspective has helped heighten awareness of the plight of children in the Third World and has also raised public and professional consciousness to the reality of child labour and child prostitution. This has been an important development, not just because it focuses attention on the plight of children in the Third World but also because it highlights that in some instances adults do abuse children for their sexual gratification in a way that is organised. Within Britain there is some evidence via research and criminal convictions that sexual abuse is not just about individuals acting alone, but can and does include adults acting as a group, or linked in a network, exploiting groups of children in what have come to be known as child sex rings (Wild & Wynne 1986).

1.5.0 DEFINITION IN SCOTLAND

1.5.1 The responsibility of social workers and the Social Work Department to protect children from abuse and neglect is detailed in child care legislation. It is that legislation which sets out the parameters for the intervention by the Social Work Department of the local authority. There is a statutory duty to cause inquiries to be made and to take action to protect where there is reasonable cause to suspect that a child is suffering or is likely to suffer significant harm (ref Social Work (Scotland) Act 1968). The abuse of children as opposed to the actions of adults is defined by the child care legislation rather than the legislation dealing with specific criminal offences against children. The crucial issue is whether certain actions may be harmful to the child rather than whether there is a law in existence about behaving in a certain way to children. This allows for the inclusion of "new forms" of abuse. What is being assessed is whether there is, or is likely to be, harm to the child because of a particular activity, and whether his or her parents or the person responsible for their care is acting reasonably to provide the necessary level of care and control.

1.5.2 The legislation is applied to practice via Scottish Office Guidance and Social Work Departments and other agencies involved in developing procedures for the handling of cases of children at risk. Within these arrangements problems over the categorisation of types of abuse have emerged. Definitions have not been readily agreed. This impedes the collation of reliable information on a national scale. Efforts are being made by the Social Work Services Group at the Home and Health Department of the Scottish Office to remedy this issue.

1.6.0 AN EMERGENT PHENOMENON

1.6.1 Since 1989/90 publicity has been given to discussion of "Satanic" and "Ritualistic" abuse. These terms have been used interchangeably. There have been assumptions made in their usage that they have been referring to the same identifiable phenomenon. The current state of knowledge is unsubstantive. The linking of sexual abuse with ceremonial or ritualised behaviour has provoked powerful emotions and responses. A polarisation of views, at times involving professional social workers, based on whether people are believers or non-believers in the existence of such phenomena rather than the accumulation of evidence in a measured manner with an open mind, has served to push people into separate camps.

1.6.2 *Directors of Social Work are concerned to reiterate that in a professional context the issue is not one of belief or non-belief. It is the assessment of what has happened to children and the gathering of systematic evidence to aid the establishment of a sound knowledge base.*

1.6.3 Although there is now a steady flow of articles with ritual or satanic abuse in the title, few papers bear academic scrutiny or constitute disciplined research (Kay & Klein (undated), Coons 1986, Davies (undated)). Consequently, caution has to be exercised in making generalisations from what in many instances are reports of a number of case examples. Yet such case examples serve a function. If they can be substantiated and validated they form building blocks in the process of developing knowledge, and identifying and labelling a phenomenon.

1.7.0 WORKING AT THE BOUNDARIES

1.7.1 Although the definition of a concept is fundamental to the establishment of a sound knowledge base, there remain considerable problems in arriving at a clear and comprehensive definition of child abuse. There are complexities related to the nature of the problem. This is particularly true in relation to sexual abuse. It is not a discrete phenomenon with clearly distinguishable characteristics but represents one extreme of a range of behaviours towards children. It is also clear that Kempe, the doctor who identified the Battered Baby Syndrome, may have been somewhat naive to suggest that sexual abuse represented the last frontier of child abuse. Our understanding of the extent and nature of this form of exploitation and abuse of children by adults is still evolving.

1.7.2 *The purpose of highlighting the processes that influence recognition and identification of child abuse is to underline the difficulties which can face even the most competent social work practitioner in keeping abreast of both knowledge and practice in a field of child care practice subject to an unforgiving and ambivalent public scrutiny.*

1.7.3 Procedures and regulatory guidance are at best a framework within which the individual social worker must bring knowledge, experience, sound professional judgement and a high level of skill to bear on the complex task of understanding the unique circumstances of each individual child. The implication for practitioners is that they are working within a field of evolving knowledge and changing public attitudes and expectations. Often they can find themselves at the forefront of discovery without the support of established knowledge. There are also considerable implications for management and practitioners. In such circumstances practice must be informed by basic values and guided by established principles.

PART II

VALUES AND PRINCIPLES

2.1.0 INTRODUCTION

2.1.1 Social work practice is informed by a set of values and principles which is based on a respect for the uniqueness of each individual, their right to make choices and decisions about their own lives and their capacity for change and growth in a nurturing environment. As a developing profession, generally accepted values are subject to challenge and change by succeeding generations. A constant feature of the debate is the extent to which social work and social workers should seek to initiate change in society rather than contributing to the status quo by mitigating clients' difficulties rather than promoting change in the circumstances which gave rise to their problems in the first place.

2.1.2 A statement of values and principles enables a framework of professional standards to be constructed against which social work practice may be judged. Social work practice in the field of child protection cannot, and should not, be viewed on its own, as an entity separate from child care practice and other social work activity.

2.2.0 CHILD CARE SERVICES

2.2.1 Most authorities produce a clear and concise statement of the principles and values which inform the ethos of their child care services. As is the case with child protection procedural guidelines, there is variation in the presentation and content of child care statements in authorities across Scotland. In many authorities there are in existence a number of well-presented policy papers on various aspects of child care services: Residential Care; Strategies for Young People in Trouble; Children with Special Needs; Work with Young People in Areas of Deprivation, etc. It is evident, however, that there is a high degree of commonality in core statements of values and principles, which include:

- ***a child's parents should be regarded as having rights and responsibilities in relation to the care of the child;***
- ***where there is conflict between the interests of parents and children, the welfare of the child is paramount;***
- ***a child should be treated as an individual;***
- ***a child has a right to safety, and adequate physical, emotional and social care;***
- ***a child has the right to have his or her needs understood and to have his or her views taken into account in planning for the child's future welfare;***
- ***a child's parents or carers should be consulted in planning for the child's future welfare;***
- ***services should be directed towards supporting and helping the family as a unit to prevent the need for children to be received into care;***
- ***if a child is to be received into care a family setting is preferable unless a comprehensive assessment indicates that this is contrary to the child's best interests;***

- ***brothers and sisters, received into care, should be placed together unless comprehensive assessment indicates that this would be contrary to their best interests;***
- ***children have a right to education and opportunities for learning social and personal skills commensurate with their needs and interests;***
- ***children have a right to health care to meet their needs and optimise their development;***
- ***if a child is received into care, his or her cultural and religious background should be respected;***
- ***reception into care should be planned and should be part of a longer term plan to return the child home;***
- ***if a return home does not prove to be a viable option, the child should be provided with permanent substitute family care.***

2.2.2 For the small group of young people whose needs, for significant periods of time, are most appropriately met within a residential setting, the Association of Directors of Social Work (ADSW), in its "Model Guidelines for the Registration and Inspection of Residential and other Establishments" (1988), recommends that specific rights should be enforceable. Such rights include:

- ***the right to individual respect;***
- ***the right to privacy and private space;***
- ***the right of access to family members (within any existing legal constraints);***
- ***specific rights related to the young person's status in care;***
- ***and, importantly, the right to a complaints appeals procedure instituted to deal with circumstances in which children believe that their rights are being withheld.***

2.3.0 PROCEDURAL GUIDANCE

2.3.1 Social work agencies, in their child care policy statements, place the highest priority on the protection of children and this is translated into procedural guidance to practice in all Regions. Whilst there are variations of detail relating to local circumstances, all procedures refer to the need for the child to be seen as soon as possible on receipt of information alleging that a child may have been abused or may be at risk of abuse. Similarly, the uniqueness of each child is reflected in the practice of placing each individual child's name on a child protection register.

The Association of Directors of Social Work, a professional organisation having in membership all senior staff in Social Work Departments in Scotland has commissioned a survey of Scottish Child Protection Registers 1990-91 by D A Gough, Senior Research Fellow, Public Health Research Unit, University of Glasgow. The study is reproduced in full as Part IX of this study.

2.3.2 Making comparisons between child protection registrations across different regions is rendered difficult on account of variations in registration categories and criteria. However, the Child Protection Steering Group on Management Information (Social Work Services Group) is currently piloting a method of gathering child protection information in different parts of Scotland, an integral part of which is consistent registration criteria. The Steering Group is aiming for the system to be applied nationally in Scotland as of April 1992.

2.3.3 ***Child abuse procedures/guidelines are intended to provide a framework within which experienced social work practitioners make judgements about the needs and risks relating to individual children and families. Most social workers find well written procedural guidelines supportive of their practice.***

2.3.4 Overly prescriptive procedures run the risk of impeding good work rather than enabling it. They risk prescribing roles for social workers to the detriment of professional discretion and judgement and some guidelines have been influenced, disproportionately, by the findings of inquiries into a small sample of child abuse cases. Whilst child protection procedures can focus the work of social workers, implicit with such labelling of the social workers' role is that they, rather than parents, carry the primary responsibility. It is, therefore, important that the responsibility for children is firmly anchored in a recognition and respect for the interests of children and their families.

2.3.5 Across Scotland, however, child protection procedures contain specific statements which are essential to good practice, which include:

- ***children should be protected from avoidable harm;***
- ***child protection investigations must be given priority over all other work;***
- ***child protection investigations must be initiated without delay;***
- ***the child should be seen and the parents interviewed;***
- ***the primary consideration is the immediate protection of the child;***
- ***child protection is an inter-agency responsibility although the police and social work departments have specific statutory responsibilities;***
- ***in the investigation of an allegation of abuse against a child, the position of other children in the household should always be considered.***

2.3.6 It is in the nature of procedural guidelines that they should be written in a style which is clear to their readership and is consistent with values underpinning childcare rather than needlessly repeating such values. It is emphasised that child protection practice should not be viewed in isolation from the principles and ethos of the authority's general child care service.

2.3.7 In relative terms it is a straightforward task to make principled statements as to what the key elements of child care policy – including child protection policy – should be. It is another matter to translate policy into practice, and subject it to evaluation against a backdrop of resource restraint and the inevitable competing demands on social workers' time.

2.3.8 *Statements of values and principles are an essential foundation to the construction of policies or strategies involving services to children and their families. But they also have an important place in informing practice in areas of work where knowledge is new and often incomplete. The circulation of clear concise statements available to all staff might assist those working in these vulnerable areas of professional activity.*

PART III

SOCIAL WORK PRACTICE

3.1.0 INTRODUCTION

3.1.1 Child protection is part of general family support work undertaken by social work staff for thousands of families throughout Scotland. There are clear principles, guidelines and statutory provisions laid down in child protection work which are designed to protect the interests and rights of children and families.

3.1.2 Investigation of child sexual abuse is part of general child protection work and the same principles, legal frameworks and guidelines have to be followed. Child sexual abuse does, however, present some different challenges. The investigation of allegations or grounds for suspicion of sexual abuse involving children from more than one family, or more than one adult perpetrator acting in concert or communication with one another, presents an even greater challenge. Nevertheless, the general principles underlying child protection work, need to inform practice in order to safeguard the rights and interests of children, families and professional helpers.

3.1.3 Social work practice in child protection in Scotland is firmly rooted in legislative and statutory requirements set out in the Social Work (Scotland) Act 1968 and is influenced by the guidance issued by the Scottish Office in Effective Intervention: Guidance on Co-operation in Scotland (HMSO, 1989).

3.1.4 Under Section 12 of the 1968 Act, Scottish local authorities have the power to promote social welfare by making available, as appropriate, advice, guidance, and assistance to children and persons in need. This general welfare principle has been reinforced by the recommendations of the Review of Child Care Law in Scotland, that assistance should be available for children:

- to support the care of the child within his/her community by provision of a range of support services, including arrangements for respite care;
- to prevent the breakdown of a family and allow children to be cared for within the community;
- to provide advice, services, and assistance to secure a child's rehabilitation for a period in care.

3.1.5 Child abuse, in all or any of its forms, is not a discrete phenomenon. The term incorporates many unacceptable ends of a wide range of behavioural responses shown towards children. There is, however, a continuing and evolving problem about choosing adequate words to describe accurately the behaviour under consideration. As differing forms of child abuse are described, it could be that principles of practice may need to be qualified or modified in their application.

3.1.6 The skills, techniques and knowledge base required for child protection work with children and families are not significantly different from those required for the full range of child care work with children and families in the community.

3.1.7 For the most part social workers, skilled and experienced in work with children and families, will have competence to deal with the investigation and management of child abuse cases. That is not to deny that child abuse work requires skills, techniques and knowledge to be effective within established criteria and structures. It is to emphasise that the well-established skills of child and family work including communicating with children and establishing honest dialogue with their parents and significant others are of equal relevance to the particular forms of work with children and families required under child protection duties.

3.1.8 Training and other forms of preparation and support for staff expected to perform child protection duties need to reflect this placement within the wider sphere of child and family work. It must also be acknowledged that some social workers may, both for professional and personal reasons, feel unable or unprepared for work in the most complex cases in this field.

3.2.0 INVESTIGATION AND EVALUATION

3.2.1 Under Section 37 of the Social Work (Scotland) Act 1968, as amended by Section 85 of the Children Act 1975, local authorities have a duty to cause inquiries to be made where information is received suggesting a child may be in need of compulsory measures of care.

3.2.2 In all Regions in Scotland, this duty is considered a matter of priority in work allocation. Therefore, duty systems and emergency out-of-hours services have been set up to respond on the same day to allegations of physical abuse or neglect.

3.2.3 Although child protection practice is dependent on inter-agency co-operation from a very early stage of recognition through to the execution of protection plans (Stevenson, 1989), the social work task in investigating child abuse needs to be distinct and is set out in the following pages.

3.2.4 Guidelines and procedures are applied by all authorities where there is need to assess whether the child is being or has been abused within the family context. There are differences throughout Scotland about the extent to which child protection procedures should be routinely applied if the child has been abused by someone outwith the family. In some authorities, for example Strathclyde and Lothian, child protection and assessment procedures are only set in process if there is a prima facie basis for concern that the child's parents cannot protect the child. In some other authorities, irrespective of who has abused the child, guidelines require social work to initiate a social work assessment with the process being halted at any stage when it is clear that the child is protected within his/her family.

3.2.5 For all authorities, helping families deal with the aftermath of abuse, assessing the possible longer term emotional damage to the child and ensuring that appropriate help is made available are part of the social work task.

3.2.6 In cases where abuse has occurred, but the identity of the perpetrator is unknown, the distinction between "child protection" procedures and general family support work can be less clear: an open mind and an ability to move from one process to the other depending on a good assessment is crucial.

3.2.7 In most Scottish authorities an immediate response is expected on receipt of referrals of physical abuse or neglect. Both research and a number of child death inquiries have indicated that minor physical injuries or neglect can be a precursor to very serious or even fatal assault.

3.2.8 In situations where there is evidence or allegation of neglect there may be a need for immediate protective action to prevent further deterioration of the child's condition to protect them from harm, or because there is no carer to be responsible for the child's care. Sadly, for some children who have been the victims of physical abuse, immediate intervention may be required to provide medical treatment. Even in cases of apparently minor injuries, a same-day assessment greatly facilitates an accurate evaluation of the cause and provides a sound basis upon which to conduct a child protection investigation. Delay can either cause further harm, risk to children or jeopardise a full and accurate assessment of the child's need for protection.

3.2.9 Some referrals of sexual abuse will also require a prompt urgent intervention. Children who have been physically harmed or traumatised as a result of penetration, or attempts at penetration, may require urgent medical assistance. In rare situations where the child's account and the contextual evidence or circumstances enable an unequivocal judgement to be made, intervention should not be delayed. However, in most sexual abuse referrals there is little overt physical evidence of abuse and concerns have usually arisen in a more indirect way. Such referrals, or more generalised expressions of concern, require a consideration of pieces of information from varying sources and a careful assessment of patterns of behaviour. Emotional abuse, because of its nature, may require a similar response.

3.2.10 *The time taken in assembling such patterns of information and co-ordinating work with the agencies has to be weighed against the possible risks of continued/repeated abuse on the one hand, or, on the other hand, to prematurely alerting the perpetrator to professional concern. To act prematurely, without the information upon which to secure a professional judgement and sustain action open to legal challenge, can leave an abused child even more vulnerable.*

3.3.0 JOINT WORKING – SOCIAL WORK AND THE POLICE

3.3.1 The response to information which suggests that a child or young person may have been abused, or may be at risk of abuse, involves precise and careful planning among Police, Social Work, Health, Education and other agencies. Given that the primary investigative task falls to police and social work, it is essential that differences in the roles and responsibilities of the two agencies do not influence, negatively, child and family-centred investigations. On the one hand, joint work may be prejudiced if the interests of the child victim are subjugated to the primacy of collecting and collating evidence for a criminal charge. On the other hand, children are often left vulnerable because of the absence of a statutory basis for working with the family. In practice, events are rarely clear-cut; for example research into a number of sexual abuse cases in three Scottish authorities demonstrates that "grey area" cases form the majority of referrals whereby uncertainty as to whether sexual abuse occurred remains at a high level (Carnie and Waterhouse).

3.3.2 In response to the dilemmas mentioned above, some authorities in Scotland promote co-ordination of child protection investigations by way of procedural guidelines which encourage staff to initiate preliminary inter-agency discussion and planning. By doing so, social work, police and other relevant agencies may gather further information and decide upon the course of action to be followed.

3.3.3 In all authorities in Scotland there are numerous examples of qualitatively high levels of practice between members of area social work teams and local police colleagues. Formal arrangements for joint investigative work between the two agencies, however, vary across the country from areas with well established schemes to areas in which formalised relationships are under discussion. At chief officer level, dialogue is generally constructive and reflects a commitment to promote joint collaborative work. There is more work to be done to arrive at a position whereby stated commitment is translated into practice. Clearly, the provision of a satisfactory and consistent standard of inter-agency practice across Scotland has major resource – including training – implications.

3.3.4 The investigation of a single allegation of child abuse within a family is frequently complex and always testing of the professional response. Investigations of allegations which involve many children and, perhaps, several adults present social work and police with particularly complex and wide-ranging difficulties. *Directors of Social Work recommend that the Scottish Office considers establishing a working group including experienced practitioners tasked to prepare guidance for both agencies as a matter of urgency and to build upon the general advice recently issued in England and Wales.*

3.4.0 TRIGGERING THE RESPONSE

3.4.1 Signs, symptoms and concerns that may be indicative of one or other form of child abuse or neglect can arise in many different ways. Social workers do not search for abused children, but because of frequent contact with children and people who care for children in many different childcare settings, attention is drawn to the circumstances of children who display worrying behaviour which could indicate child abuse. It is, therefore, integral to Scottish child protection procedures that possible signs and symptoms are set out to enable staff to follow up concerns and to ensure that a child is not experiencing unnecessary suffering or impairment to their health and development.

3.4.2 The extent to which social workers can be alert to possible signs of abuse/neglect rests on full understanding of normal child health and development. Teaching about the normal development of children is a prerequisite of professional social work training.

3.4.3 Not all information indicating the possibility of sexual abuse comes from reliable sources. There can often be a lengthy communication path from victim, to friend, to friend's parent, to relatives, to police. It is always important, therefore, to sift information to clarify the identity of the alleged perpetrator and establish his/her whereabouts. Other information about the child, the family, and the child's health, social and educational development will all be relevant considerations. In many authorities it is now established practice that on referral of an incident of alleged abuse, consideration will be given to the appropriateness of checking existing records for relevant information and considering the timing of any further investigation or intervention. Checks are made with relevant health, educational and social work personnel and of the Child Protection Register to establish any existing concern about the child's safety. Indeed, one of the original purposes of Child Protection Registers (LASSL (80) 4, London) was to prevent the loss or fragmentation of crucial information which could have a bearing on a child's safety.

3.4.4 The timescale for carrying out this preparatory work is brief and must never delay immediate protective action, but is considered necessary to prevent precipitate intrusion into children's and families' lives.

3.4.5 *In situations in which the allegation, or matters which give rise to concern, involve children from more than one family, or suggest that the adult or adults involved may be acting in concert with others or be linked by a network, there is a risk that social workers may hold back from the standard practice of interagency collaboration because of the extent of the links involved, and the possibilities of professionals being involved in the abusive activities. Recent well-publicised cases exampling the involvement of staff from health and social work settings establish the basis of such apprehensions where children from more than one family are involved in alleged abuse or where parents may be acting in concert with others or linked by a network.*

3.4.6 People who abuse children can come from all walks of life, including the professions. There can be significant risk to children if assumptions are made in particular cases where more that one adult may be involved if standard interagency collaboration is jettisoned because of a generalised concern about the involvement of professionals. Obviously caution must apply when there is any evidence, however uncorroborated, that such involvement could be in question.

3.4.7 The investigative task in an island community is a particularly sensitive one. Professionals are likely to be well-known to the community as private individuals. This will inevitably put a strain on interagency collaboration and demand extra care from professionals that they are acting and making decisions in a professional capacity. It must be acknowledged that in larger authorities there is greater choice for work to be allocated to people who have no personal connections with the children or families involved.

3.5.0 PERPETRATOR UNKNOWN

3.5.1 Where there is clear and unequivocal evidence that a child has been sexually abused, social workers and police have careful and complex decisions to make. The more so if a possible perpetrator is the natural parent who is entitled to rights in the Scottish child care legal system.

3.5.2 Ideally, assessment in these cases should occur while the child is protected within the family or community. There will be very few occasions when the risks to a child's safety are considered so great that the removal to a place of safety will be necessary to complete an assessment. Even in these circumstances, information from adult survivors of sexual abuse suggests the fear of the abuser is likely to be so overwhelming as to prevent any clear disclosure from the child. Some research studies have highlighted that a child will describe their abuse only when protected and away from their abuser (Finkelhor; Roberts et al). However, distance will not always guarantee that a child can talk. It is believed to be a feature of abuse involving more than one adult that the injunctions on a child not to speak are extremely powerful and effective (Jones, D 1991). Nevertheless, given that in over 65% of reported cases of sexual abuse to children in one Scottish region in 1989, the alleged perpetrator was not a parent or relative or step-parent, (Roberts et al, 1991), it is extremely important to take time to assess the situation and form a view on whether parent(s) or carer(s) are able to take the necessary protective action. This research has been supported by recent evidence from a retrospective study undertaken by the Polytechnic of North London (Kelly et al, 1991): 68% of reported abuse was perpetrated by distant relatives and known adults and peers.

3.5.3 The validity and sources of information about a child's alleged abuse need to be assessed very carefully. Unexpected questioning of a child who has alleged nothing to anyone could be considered harmful unless there are very strong reasons to suspect the child is in immediate danger. It seems important to emphasise the need for careful interagency assessment of the nature of information received: to stop and think and to create a system where ideas/worries/theories can be weighed up objectively in a supervised setting. This has to be an expected standard of practice in order to ensure a professional response and a protection of children's rights.

3.6.0 WORKING WITH PARENTS

3.6.1 Following the initial evaluative and preparatory stages, a standard format for the conduct of a child protection investigation should generally cover the following areas:

- arrangements must be agreed for guidance, supervision and co-ordination of the investigation;
- parents should be informed of social work activities from the outset;
- child(ren) should be seen and communicated with as appropriate;
- concerns from colleagues in primary health care services or schools should be elicited.

3.6.2 During direct contact with the child(ren) and the family, social workers should be asking questions about the details of the alleged abuse, the parent's views and the child's views. Some assessment of the validity of the parents' accounts should be made. Careful observations and assessments of the composition of the household and family communications are expected. All children in the household will be considered. An assessment of the need for medical evaluation or treatment should be made. Consideration will need to be given to the involvement of the Police.

3.6.3 Throughout the investigation, the social worker will be making judgements about the nature of any immediate physical risk, whether the child is able to communicate freely, whether the parents are co-operating with the investigation, whether one parent can take action to protect the child (if the other is the perpetrator), and the extent to involve other agencies. Often this complex task is shared with another social worker, or a police officer.

3.6.4 Key decisions have to be made about whether any child requires immediate protective action, such as the taking of a Place of Safety Order or immediate medical intervention. Full assessments need to be made about whether the risk can be removed by action involving the perpetrator, whether there is protection within the family, the extended family or close community network, before moving to substitute care.

3.6.5 It is a basic principle of natural justice and social work practice that children and families are given information about the nature of any allegation and the reasons for investigation.

3.6.6 It is therefore taken as standard practice to inform parents and children (as age appropriate) of the nature of any concerns that have been expressed and that an investigation is taking place. The vast majority of families react responsibly to this open and honest approach. There are tensions of timing when a parent is the alleged perpetrator of the abuse and the police wish to interview their suspect for criminal investigation purposes, but, generally speaking these difficulties can be overcome in joint working arrangements with the protection of the child being the paramount concern.

3.6.7 There may be a very few occasions when to inform the parents may be judged to be putting the child at risk of further abuse. Directors of Social Work propose that the criteria for not informing parents before taking protective action should be:

- parent cannot be found and child requires immediate protection;
- parent has a known history of acting out threats of violence to the child when challenged by people in authority;
- there is a soundly based professional judgement, made following an evaluation of firm information, that the parent would remove the child into hiding and out of reach of monitoring arrangements;
- where there is soundly based professional judgement, made following an evaluation of firm information, that the parent is acting with others to perpetrate offences against the child, or children, and could alert others resulting in other children being removed from assistance or abducted. It would be assumed here that there is already information about alleged abuse which has indicated definite links between the adults concerned.

3.7.0 TIMING AN INTERVENTION

3.7.1 Social Work Departments receive referrals about children at risk 24 hours a day, 365 days per year. Many emergencies arise outwith normal office hours. Risk and injury to children is commonly referred late at night when children may be reported as abandoned, or subject to violence, as a result of behaviour by adults impaired by alcohol and/or drugs. Social work practitioners react promptly to these situations, and significant numbers of children are received into care late at night or in the early hours of the morning for care or treatment or protection. The timing of intervention in these events is primarily determined by the circumstances which have placed the child at risk.

3.7.2 If intervention, such as immediate protective action, is required, any decision about timing would have to be based on individual children's needs and any special family circumstances. If children are judged to be in need of removal from the family home, preparation of and information to children and family is standard practice, as is complex negotiation about the location of a safe and appropriate placement which would minimise the potential disruption to a child's life. The removal of children from their home is the most difficult task that social workers are asked to undertake. It is traumatic for children, for parents and for the staff who have to undertake it. The situation is inevitably an emotionally charged one and if badly handled can be traumatic for everyone involved. It could be argued that, given the nature of the task, the timing and location of immediate protective action will inevitably have unsatisfactory consequences.

3.7.3 The standard principle of practice should be that extreme intervention in a child's or family's life needs to be justified by firm grounds for believing that such action is the only option available to protect the child from being abused.

3.7.4 In a few very rare cases the timing of taking protective action could be linked to factors, other than the child and family based assessment. If, for example, the parents are judged to be in communication with others who could remove their children into hiding, and in doing so place them at risk of further harm, there could possibly be a need for a precisely planned intervention to be made without any prior notice to the people involved. The timing of such an intervention should not be dictated by the evidential requirements of a criminal investigation, important as such requirements might be.

3.7.5 Circumstances may and do arise where events take place which involve social workers intervening in families to protect children late at night. These actions are precipitated by actions and decisions of the family members concerned. These episodes are qualitatively different from the situation of a planned intervention following an on-going inquiry by the Social Work Department. In such circumstances the removal of children who are sleeping in their homes or have just risen from their beds cannot be supported as a form of intervention centred on the interests of the children concerned. *In the view of Directors of Social Work the child's needs should be the predominant consideration throughout the investigation and any intervention. Interventions led by considerations related to the collection of evidence place the child's interest in a secondary position.*

3.7.6 If immediate protective action is judged not to be necessary, time will be spent on explaining the child protection system to the family, ensuring that follow-up inquiries are in place and in deciding about the need for or the planning of a case conference. If there is an assessment that the child(ren) may be in need of compulsory measures of care, a referral must be made to the Reporter to the Children's Panel as defined in Section 32 of the Social Work (Scotland) Act 1968.

3.7.7 *Directors have considered whether there are ever any occasions when the full inter-agency preparatory work can be omitted and whether the normal process of stages (1) evaluation and information collection and (2) investigation and (3) judgement about emergency protective action, should ever be over-turned and immediate protective action taken before the standard investigative stage. The normal sequence of events may well have to be reversed if:*

- *the child is clearly in immediate physical danger: for example, abandoned without a carer, or being overtly threatened by a carer with a weapon (police officers' warrants can be used in these circumstances), or if the child is in urgent need of medical care;*
- *the parent(s) are totally refusing to co-operate with statutory agencies in carrying out their statutory duties: therefore making assessment of risk to the child impossible – and intervention the only way to conduct the necessary assessment;*
- *by informing parent(s) openly of concerns, there are firm and reasonable grounds to suspect that this could put the child further at risk to life or limb.*

3.8.0 EVALUATION AND PROFESSIONAL JUDGEMENT

3.8.1 Assessing information/evidence in child sexual abuse is dependent on a firm knowledge base. What has to be recognised is that knowledge and understanding about sexual abuse in the UK is at an evolutionary stage. The accounts of adults abused as children indicate that denial is likely to be a common response. It is therefore fundamental to the investigation of child sexual abuse that "the truth" will rarely be obvious. Victims are reticent and can withdraw statements, perpetrators deny because of the implications of loss of liberty for them if they confess (Wyre 1990 and Salter 1988), family and other professional workers may deny the possibility of sexual abuse, because they do not wish to believe sexual abuse has happened to the child concerned.

3.8.2 Nevertheless, whilst the possibility of denial must be faced, no investigation should take place on the unquestioning assumption that child sexual abuse has happened: the guiding principle for all concerned should be to keep an open mind and provide an open door should further information be forthcoming. Evaluating allegations, referrals, or expressions of concern that involve children from more than one family, involve more than one adult, or involve adults acting in concert or communication can be complex. There may be situations in which parents appear unable to see the risk and protect their child, wittingly or unwittingly colluding with the perpetrator's relationship with the child, if not aiding it. Knowledge about this phenomenon or probably "these phenomena" is in its infancy. It could be argued that principles of social work practice applied to cases of sexual abuse may need to be adapted when it comes to sexual/physical abuse enacted in a different context. The possibility of there being distinctive features about abuse which is premeditated and contrived by adults acting in concert with one another needs to be allowed.

3.8.3 For the moment social workers are seeking to apply existing guidelines to areas of human behaviour which are as yet not defined or reliably described, and about which our knowledge is uncertain. "The use of specific terms such as ritualistic or satanistic abuse appears unwarranted at present until we know more about this complex topic" (Jones, 1991). Jones, currently a recognised expert in child psychiatry, has spent considerable time helping assess potential child victims of so-called "ritualistic" or "satanic" abuse or multiple victims of child sexual abuse. Jones prefers to dispense with the term "ritualistic" abuse and *in each case* "to consider the extent to which other types of abuse or multiple victims occur". Jones notes the potential for mass hysteria, the potential for jeopardising "the objectivity of practitioners". "Social contagion, or contamination, between parents and between professionals may effect the perception of events and possibly also parental and professional objectivity." (Jones 1991)

3.8.4 Until the knowledge base is more certain, and a more universal understanding and acceptance of the nature of child abuse perpetrated by adults in a planned and premeditated way is established, social workers will be faced with having to allow for the possibility of such events taking place whilst testing the evidence and being cautious in its application.

3.9.0 INTERVIEWING CHILDREN

3.9.1 If social work staff are interviewing children for the purpose of a child abuse investigation, they must be clear that this is their task. The child needs to understand the purpose of the interview, too. Some children under five and some with a handicap may not be able to understand fully why they are being interviewed: developmentally appropriate techniques have to be used.

3.9.2 It is very important to stress that an interview with an allegedly abused child is *only one part of the investigation* and must be supplemented by other assessments and multi-disciplinary inquiries. It has been suggested that "the way in which the interview with the child fits in with other parts of the multi-disciplinary process of assessment in a community must be worked out on a local basis." Such working arrangements, particularly between police and social work are now developing in Scotland. (Findlay C, 1990, Dempster and MacMillan, 1991).

3.9.3 One of the central aims of special joint police/social work initiatives has been to keep investigations of child abuse as child-centred as possible, keeping interviews and medical examinations to the minimum.

3.9.4 As joint investigation practice increases, it is essential for social work to be clear about the social work role and task in the investigation. In child protection work, social workers are the lead officers in the assessment of the need for protection of the child within the family, that is, in determining whether there is a need for compulsory measures of care. If the abuse is from outwith the family and the child is judged to be well protected, there may be a role for social work in helping the child and the family cope with the aftermath of the abuse, or even prevent its recurrence.

3.9.5 An investigation of sexual abuse is not only a criminal investigation about the act of abuse. Assessments need to be made of the child's physical, emotional and social needs, of relationships in the family, of social supports, of the family's ability to access and make use of family support services. Social workers have a key role in these decisions: a qualified social worker has a unique combination of skills and, as a local government officer, has the necessary access to resources which may be needed to protect the child.

3.9.6 The criminal investigation role is primarily one of establishing whether a crime has been committed and whether an alleged perpetrator should be prosecuted. The interviewing of victims for this purpose is the primary task of the police, but at all stages of an investigation it is important for social work staff to hold onto their primary role of investigating the need for protection of the child. Interviewing victims and carers is therefore seen as a primary social work task.

3.9.7 Given the complexities of some investigations, and the desire to protect children through successful prosecution of perpetrators, there can be tensions during a joint police/social work investigation about which is the primary task and who takes the lead role.

3.9.8 *Directors of Social Work are firmly of the view that, throughout the investigation, evaluation and intervention, the interests and needs of the child victim should predominate and the process should serve that end. The wider interests of the community are an important consideration but should not be pursued at the risk of further harm to the child who has been the victim.*

3.9.9 Often the evidence of the existence of sexual abuse can crucially depend on hearing what the child has to say: "the child's account is of prime importance" (Jones, 1989). Nonetheless, maintaining the principles of keeping the child's interests paramount, it is essential not to put pressure on any child or young person nor put them through a harmful interrogative experience.

3.9.10 There are particular challenges in identifying sexual abuse, which may not leave any medical signs (Roberts et al, 1989) and may not have been alleged by the child (Butler-Sloss, 1988). Many children who initially allege that they have been sexually abused, later retract their allegations but this does not necessarily mean that the abuse did not happen. Others have understandable and grave difficulties in giving a clear verbal story of what has happened to them (Glasgow D, 1989 and Sgroi, 1982). The emotional consequences of abuse have been well-described in work about survivors (Hall and Lloyd, 1989 and Bain, 1990). An understanding of the fear, guilt, shame and self-hatred that a child sexual abuse victim can suffer is necessary to facilitate children telling about sexual abuse in a way that avoids further blame or condemnation for the victim.

3.9.11 It is important to acknowledge that individual work with a child, with a view to helping a child speak about sexual abuse, cannot be undertaken unless the purpose is out in the open. The phrase "*disclosure work*", still used by many health and social work professionals, is both an unhelpful and unwise description of the process because of the danger of assuming that a child with problems definitely has something to disclose. If therapeutic work with a child produces a spontaneous description of sexual abuse, as not uncommonly happens in child psychiatric practice (Kolvin *et al*, 1988), then it is essential to move to a clear investigative mode, properly staffed and recorded for evidential purposes.

3.9.12 In order to be able to achieve sensitive interviewing of children in such a difficult and complex area, staff need to be able to communicate well with children in most contexts. The basic minimum standards Directors expect from staff in communicating with children would be to have a knowledge of "normal" child development and behaviour in the age-range with which the worker is concerned. Some staff in family centres or residential units who do not have formal professional qualifications may be the people children choose to confide in. Staff need a general level of competence in knowledge and skills related to children, and ability to view things from the child's perspective – to see their starting-point, their view of what is happening to them and their family – and help them express their worries. Staff would be expected to have at their disposal age-appropriate materials and resources for helping a child or young person to express their thoughts: this could vary from dolls and play-people for young children to the use of rock music and spraypaint for older kids. Children and young people do not talk like adults, are unlikely to respond to questioning in the same way as adults and are especially wary of strangers and people in authority. Some children are over-compliant with adults and it is important not to exploit them.

3.9.13 Following recent legislation in England and Wales (Criminal Evidence Act, 1990) that permits the showing of video evidence in court, draft Home Office guidelines (1991) have been produced which propose the use of a clear framework for interviewing children who may have been abused. The guidelines follow the "stepwise" approach to interviewing, which recommends that the interviewer moves in a relatively set process from general open questioning to more direct and specific questions. The guidelines are intended to help professionals and victims to produce a video-recording of an investigative interview which will stand the test required for criminal rather than civil proceedings. It is important to recognise the potential dangers to a child of a poorly conducted interview which can be thrown out of court because of, for example, leading questions. The guidelines will greatly assist practice in investigative interviews.

3.9.14 Nevertheless, it is important for the social work and legal professions and the public to recognise that investigative interviews are only a small part of "communicating with" troubled children. Children and young people do not choose to talk in a perfect setting for an accurate video-recording. Many will choose to speak spontaneously, out of office hours, to people such as foster parents with whom they feel secure. It is important that staff remain mindful of the small proportion of cases which are likely to be dealt with in criminal proceedings and, therefore, understand clearly the basis of the standard test of evidence in civil proceedings in Scotland based on the "balance of probabilities".

3.9.15 General principles for communicating with children should, therefore, include an ability to relate to children and young people, to use resources and equipment that are age-appropriate, to be able to proceed at a child's pace and to be conscious of the fact that in an interview the adult has power.

3.10.0 SPECIALIST SOCIAL WORK PRACTITIONERS

3.10.1 Directors acknowledge the variation in social work opinion in different parts of Scotland regarding the value of appointing specialist social work practitioners in the field of child protection.

3.10.2 Directors wish to emphasise that for the most part social workers with skill and experience in work with children and families will be competent to deal with the investigation and management of child abuse cases. By firmly placing investigative and post-investigative work in the domain of experienced social work practitioners:

- arrangements may be made for in-service and post-qualifying training;
- specialist consultation and support may be offered;
- child protection work remains within the context of child care;
- the potential disruption for children and families of having contact with an investigating social worker and, thereafter, a social worker carrying out post-investigative work is eliminated;
- the particular difficulties for small authorities in gaining access to a specialist worker are eliminated;
- recognition is given to the fact that most children who inform about abuse do not inform social workers in the first place. (Roberts, Dempster and Taylor)

3.10.3 However, a number of authorities and practitioners favour the appointment of specialist social workers to undertake work in the field. Those favouring more specialised models of service and practice would lay stress on the following factors:

- too little time in professional training and supervised practice is spent on child-orientated work;
- specialisation leads to increased knowledge, expertise and professional satisfaction;
- specialists are available on a consultative and advisory basis for colleagues;
- the complexity of the overall demands on social work agencies means that specialisation is inevitable if workers are to keep up-to-date with developments in practice;
- investigations by specialists serve as a check to the views of, for example, social workers already working with families;
- other staff are freed from the immediacy of having to respond to child protection referrals and, therefore, disruption to other child care tasks is reduced;
- investigative work with the police is enhanced by reducing the number of social workers involved in joint work;

- specialism at the investigative stage results in a more informed understanding of the hierarchy of evidential needs and a clearer focus on the distinction between evaluative and therapeutic interventions.

3.10.4 Directors recognise that there are sound arguments on both sides of the specialist debate and do not advocate the use of one model over another. Arguments for or against the use of specialist social workers in child protection cannot be viewed in an organisational vacuum, and in this sense some authorities more than others adopt specialist models in the delivery of their social work services to specific client groups. Furthermore, the use of specialist social workers must also be seen in the context of developed, or developing, working relationships with the police and the achievement of meaninful collaborative practice. It will be for each authority to adopt the arrangements for the deployment of skilled staff which are best suited to the needs of the community it serves. Local authorities' training programmes will need to reflect the model of service that they have chosen to adopt.

3.11.0 THE ROLE OF PSYCHOLOGISTS AND CHILD PSYCHIATRISTS

3.11.1 The professional literature on child abuse and neglect highlights other professionals, particularly child psychiatrists, paediatricians and child psychologists who have a wealth of knowledge and experience to offer in cases of alleged child abuse. Section 37 of the Social Work (Scotland) Act 1968 states that the Social Work Department has a statutory duty to "cause inquiries to be made". The skills and expertise of other professionals can have an important part to play in evaluating the issues and deciding what course to take.

3.11.2 The role particularly of child psychiatry and specialist educational or clinical psychologists in the investigation of sexual abuse of children is contentious. Many such professionals regard their primary professional function as therapists rather than investigators or even assessors (see for example, the statement made by the Child Sexual Abuse Team at Dundee Royal Infirmary). Some authors such as Jones, Bain, Will, Wynne and Hobbs are used as experts because of their development of personal skills and interest in cases of sexual abuse, in addition to their professional knowledge and experience.

3.11.3 Paediatricians, child psychiatrists and psychologists can have a significant contribution to make in the assessment and treatment of abused children. What is required is a confident social work system which is able to identify cases where the other professionals would have something beneficial to offer the child and the family beyond the skills or competence of the social work team. This statement corresponds with the view published by The Independent Second Opinion Panel to the Cleveland Inquiry (British Journal of Hospital Medicine, 1988) "Social Service Departments, paediatricians, and/or police surgeons and child psychiatrists will all have major roles; different but related, in the assessment of child sexual abuse at a clinical level." This view is endorsed by a recent paper published by the British Psychological Society (1990). "Although psychology has a unique contribution to make, this contribution must be made in collaboration with other professionals .... one important task for psychologists is to become more aware of the expertise and different objectives of other professionals. (British Psychological Society, 1990)

3.11.4 These views can best be summarised by a working group of the Child and Adolescent Specialist Section of the Royal College of Psychiatrists:

"In some cases the referrer is not requesting an assessment of the child's psychiatric state, but is asking whether the psychiatrist thinks that sexual abuse has occurred. In general this type of referral is more appropriately dealt with by social services and/or police departments, especially where there is already a high likelihood of child sexual abuse. There are some situations where the child psychiatrist may wish to take on a diagnostic role, after consultation with social services and/or police colleagues, because of other factors if a very young child who is barely able to talk, a mentally handicapped child .... a child who is severely psychiatrically disturbed. In some circumstances the child psychiatrist may be the person with the appropriate skills and expertise to discuss questions of abuse with the child and in these circumstances the benefit of assessment skills should not be withheld." (Royal College, 1988)

3.11.5 The use of these specialist resources needs to be related to cases which present special or complex features. Even then there is a wide variation in practice of the extent to which individual consultants are willing or have the experience to make an authoritative contribution to the assessment or evaluation.

3.12.0 CONTRACTING OUT THE TASK OF EVALUATION

3.12.1 The issue of access to and availability of social workers with higher levels of training and skill, together with access to specialists with recognised expertise from other professions, can pose significant problems in island authorities and sparsely populated rural areas.

3.12.2 Circumstances can arise where assistance is sought from other authorities, professions or voluntary organisations. Given the primary responsibility of the initiating local authority in respect of its statutory duty, the nature of any contract needs to be clarified in terms of professional practice and judgement as well as economic terms.

3.12.3 The extent to which the authority initiating the request for assistance is entitled to rely upon the competence, judgement and advice of those who are acting as its agents needs to be clarified. Authorities should be able to rely on professional competence if they seek and appoint experienced professionals as their agents. However, judgements about intervention rest with the commissioning authority which must weigh any advice or opinion offered by its agents against a test of reasonableness, an understanding of its statutory duty, the needs of the child(ren) and knowledge of its local community.

3.12.4 Advice and opinions can assist the local authority to carry through its statutory responsibility, though it is important to emphasise that tensions can arise if medical or psychiatric consultants perceive a conflict between their professional responsibility to the child as their client and the local authority's statutory responsibility.

3.13.0 RECORDING INFORMATION GATHERED

3.13.1 It is still a matter of considerable debate whether or not the use of videotapes in recording interviews or sessions with children will facilitate either the interviewing of children or the subsequent presentation in law. The Pigot report (1989) made firm recommendations about the use of pre-trial videos, but there are many reservations about the advisability of the general use of videos. Many social workers hold the view that children should have the right to refuse to have their descriptions of very personal, private pain put on film. Some children may have been used for the purposes of pornography and therefore video-recording could rekindle memories of earlier abuse. Another serious concern is that there may not be enough safeguards to protect exploitation or even misuse of video material by defence counsel in criminal cases. (MacFarland and Waterman, 1986, and O'Hara M, 1991). Another consideration is that the requirements of fixed filming equipment and high quality reproduction (often needing a skilled technician), could conflict with the need to hold an interview that is child-sensitive and not dominated by any pressure for perfect film reproduction.

3.13.2 One of the current challenges is to improve and consolidate social work practice in investigating child sexual abuse and in devising guidelines for social work staff and other workers. As noted by one of the most experienced workers in America, "If you require that there be corroboration of the child's story by physical evidence, witnesses, or a confession by the perpetrator, you will turn many cases into "non-cases". Corroborating physical evidence or witnesses are rare. Perpetrators hardly ever confess ...." (Sgroi 1982).

3.13.3 In the view of Directors of Social Work all staff should be advised to record in writing, immediately after the interview, the essential statements made by the child, observations of behaviour/distress that are relevant to the interview, any opinions that cannot be substantiated at present but may provide material for further inquiry, and then establish with the child what the interviewer has understood from the interview and where, if anywhere, that information will go. It is important that social workers are clear about the differing tests of evidential requirements between establishing a case for the purpose of child protection (on the balance of probabilities) and providing evidence for a criminal conviction (beyond all reasonable doubt).

3.13.4 Much dependence can be put on establishing "the credibility of child's story". It is a general practice wisdom or consensus that there are elements to a child's story which lend validation to the allegations. These cover:

(a) *Context of the abuse* – the child can give details of clothes, location, what was said, when the abuse happened, and will be able to describe sensory experiences that are difficult to fabricate.

(b) *A description of the behaviour* – explicit descriptions of sexual behaviour, knowledge of sexual behaviour beyond that expected for the child's development stage and a description from the child's viewpoint using that child's understanding and language, e.g. "he sucked my manny like a lolly".

(c) *Emotional reactions* – considered consistent with a true allegation are "avoidance of a discussion of the abuse, depression, anger, embarrassment, fear, disgust, anxiety and sexual arousal" (Faller, 1988). It is also quite indicative of a true allegation that a description is faltering, or conveys a progression of sexual activity over time (Morrison et al, 1987). An understanding of a child's emotional reactions is dependent on a clear picture of the child's age and development. More very young children are able to be straight forward about the abuse because of their lack of sophistication. Older children and teenagers are frequently more aware of the implications and consequences of what they have to tell.

3.13.5 The dilemmas which face staff were well described by Anne Hollows from the Child Abuse Training Unit at the National Children's Bureau: "Certainties are few in this work and professional maturity is needed to tolerate uncertainty and manage risk, for both the child and the worker. Investigative work with children who may have been abused requires social workers to analyse often contradictory information, emotions, responses and clues, and process them in the light of knowledge and experience." Social workers continue to be responsible for children where there is no clear story or evidence, and need to continue to work with the child to pursue the best way to help that child and family.

3.14.0 JOINT WORKING WITH HEALTH AND OTHER DISCIPLINES

3.14.1 In all cases of abuse and neglect it is considered essential to collaborate with the appropriate health personnel. Careful medical evaluation in some cases of abuse, e.g. multiple fractures of different ages, bite marks, non-organic failure to thrive, ingestion of poisons, is essential to establish non-accidental causes of the abuse. Careful examination over a period of time by paediatric personnel is necessary to establish developmentally deleterious effects of neglect. It is also standard practice to have a medical examination on reception into care with the child's, young person's or parent's agreement.

3.14.2 The best interests of children and young people will be served by ensuring the avoidance of unnecessary or repeated medical examinations. The drive to secure a criminal conviction should not be a determining factor in assessing whether or not a child needs to be medically examined. Consequently when collecting information or investigating allegations of abuse, police and social workers need to establish whether or not there is evidence, in the particular circumstances under investigation, that indicates a medical examination is necessary. Such principles are recommended by Butler-Sloss (1988) and are dependent on good local joint working arrangements with police, health and social work personnel.

3.14.3 Awareness of abuse or neglect is not just the responsibility of social work professionals, however, and it is heartening to read the SED guidelines for teaching staff (SED, 1990) which endorse the statement on inter-agency working:
"Child abuse is not – the preserve of any one public or voluntary service." "The starting point of the child protection system in Scotland is that any person who has a knowledge or a reasonable suspicion that a child is being abused or is at risk of abuse should communicate their concern ...." (Effective Intervention).

3.14.4 Given the possibilities of even larger groups of professionals being included in the investigation of multiple or organised abuse, the need for supervision, consultation, and co-ordination is even greater. Scottish authorities perhaps should consider the special appointment of an overall consultant/co-ordinator in these cases to prevent mis-communication and fragmentation when clear goals and tasks need to be set for each worker and each child.

3.15.0 CASE CONFERENCES

3.15.1 A case conference involves calling together professionals from different disciplines and agencies to share information and to focus on the needs of a particular client or family. Such conferences are a long established professional practice in social work and are used in other disciplines where there is a need to co-ordinate service responses. The case conference is a mechanism used when problems are complex, when information held by more than one profession or agency needs to be shared, when there is a need to co-ordinate activity to achieve specified outcomes, or to collate information to arrive at a balanced judgement. Since the early 1970s case conferences have been identified as a critical mechanism for sharing information, co-ordinating work between agencies in the field of child abuse and taking important decisions about children in a collaborative way.

3.15.2 The importance of well-attended and effectively conducted case conferences has been a central tenet of advice and guidance given to local authorities by central government in Scotland as in England and Wales. Significant changes in the detail of central government advice have taken place over the past five to six years. In the late seventies and early eighties the emphasis from government was on using case conferences to collate information and plan strategies and interventions to secure the protection of children. Advice from the Department of Health in 1986 stated:

"It is not appropriate for parents to attend case conferences which are professional meetings focusing on the details of inter-agency co-operation to protect the child and plan for the future."

3.15.3 The separation of a large number of children, believed to have been sexually abused, from their parents in Cleveland in 1987 gave rise to widespread public concern. The decision-making processes adopted by professionals, including case conferences, were scrutinised in the subsequent Inquiry. The importance of obtaining information from parents to assist the process of formulating professional judgements was highlighted. Plans made by case conferences had long-term consequences both for the interests of children and the rights of parents. The publication of the Report of the Inquiry into Child Abuse in Cleveland in 1987 coincided with wider public concerns about Access to Information and a greater openness and accountability in the decision-making of public authorities.

3.15.4 The Report of the Inquiry into Child Abuse in Cleveland emphasised the importance of eliciting information from parents and ensuring that any indicators, suspicions or allegations were evaluated in the context of a thorough knowledge and understanding of the child's relationship with its parents and the home circumstances. Following the recommendations of the Inquiry report, new guidance on case conferences was issued by the Department of Health in 1988:

"Parents should be invited, where practicable, to attend part or, if appropriate, the whole of case conferences unless in the view of the chair, their presence precludes consideration of the child's interests."

This advice is endorsed by the most recent advice issued to Social Work Departments by the Social Work Services Group in a document entitled "Effective Intervention", 1990.

3.15.5 It is now deemed good practice to invite parents to participate at case conferences. Indeed social workers risk severe criticism if they do not make efforts to involve parents in the process (Rochdale Report). The philosophy underpinning the notion of parental participation at case conferences reflects that espoused in the Children Act 1989 in England and Wales. Respect and responsibility are emphasised as key concepts in openness and honesty between professional and parent, thus creating an effective engagement to work for change.

3.15.6 The introduction of this new policy into practice has not been without its tensions. Some professionals feel uncomfortable facing parents directly with their concerns for fear it will lead to upset and repercussions, eg the child being taken out of school and moved to another school if a teacher or Head is perceived to be the origin of concerns about a child's well-being. The involvement of parents can pose problems for the Police who often consider that the presence of parents can inhibit their contribution, particularly when there is a prosecution in prospect and the parent who is the accused is present. Medical practitioners and social workers may also experience a dilemma about involving parents if the parents' interests are perceived to run counter to what is in the best interests of the child.

3.15.7 The process of involving parents in case conferences is complex. Their presence can have a significant impact on the openness with which professionals share information, express opinions and test hypotheses and judgements with one another. Case conferences involving parents can only hope to be purposeful and constructive if the conference has a skilled and experienced chairperson able to hold the confidence of all participants, enable each to make a relevant contribution and not lose sight of the fact that the outcome of the conference is to promote the interests of the child(ren).

3.15.8 Across Scotland that practice and pattern of involving parents in case conferences varies considerably. In some local authorities practice guidelines require that a case conference takes place within 48 hours, in others within 7 days, of a referral. Such differences suggest that the role and function of case conferences varies from authority to authority and that before the question of involving parents can be properly addressed, authorities need to clarify their procedures.

3.15.9 The use of an initial case conference/case discussion between agencies within 24-48 hours of the receipt of a referral is essential to gathering information and formulating further lines of inquiry. It enables agreement between agencies as to how parents are to be approached if they are not already involved and how any strengths, risks or vulnerability in the child's family background are to be evaluated.

3.15.10 This initial process can also be conducted by discussion and agreement between agencies and workers without the formal requirement to meet as a case conference/case discussion. It is a critically important piece of communication and co-ordination. Failure to do it properly and thoroughly and at the right time can have, and has had, serious life-threatening consequences for too many children for the lesson not to be learnt.

3.15.11 The process of co-ordinating the gathering of information and co-ordinating further investigation is separate and distinct from the process of collating that information, and arriving at a balanced professional judgement about the needs of the child in both the short and long-term. The security/danger presented to the child's interests by parents are central and critical to the judgement which professionals must exercise in recommending the statutory agencies to exercise powers within the law to protect children. The attendance of parents at case conferences to ensure that account is taken of their views in the exercise of a professional judgement about the welfare of children is, therefore, central to the context of the decision-making process. The nature of the parents' involvement in the process will be qualified by the circumstances. A parent of whom there are reasonable grounds for suspecting that they have abused a child sexually or physically should be offered the opportunity to be heard. It would clearly not be in the interests of the child for that parent to participate in the process of deciding the arrangements for the child's further care. The views, abilities, strengths and contribution of a non-abusing parent may be the single most significant factor in deciding the child's future care.

3.15.12 The present inconsistent patterns of parental involvement in case conferences need to be addressed in further work by the Scottish Office to develop consistent and positive guidance to all agencies involved: Health, Police, Education and Social Work. Authorities need to review their own local guidelines for practice and ensure that the arrangements for inter-agency co-ordination of investigations and the role of case conferences is clear and unambiguous.

3.15.13 The critical contribution of the person who chairs or contributes to the issues related to the involvement of parents will need to be addressed in training programmes. Social workers will need training to prepare both parents and themselves for parents' involvement in case conferences. Inter-agency training programmes should also reflect the issues which will need to be addressed to involve parents.

3.15.14 It would be helpful to professional staff and parents to consider the preparation of an information leaflet on the conduct of child abuse investigations and procedures. Whilst such a leaflet cannot release parents from the anxiety inevitably associated with the process, at least they would have an understanding of the procedures in outline.

PART IV

TRAINING

4.1.0 INTRODUCTION

4.1.1 There is universal acceptance that the quality of work undertaken with children and families by the staff of Social Work Departments can be improved by greater investment in training. Over the past three decades the Government has found resources to support costly public inquiries but has been reluctant to provide resources to invest in training. There was some change in this position in 1989 when specific grants were introduced to improve the quality of training in child abuse in both England and Wales. Only very recently has the Minister of State responsible for the Home and Health Department indicated his intention to introduce such arrangements in Scotland and the issue as to whether this would be "new money" has as yet to be clarified.

4.1.2 The responsibilities of Social Work Departments and the needs of children and their families are such that there are currently many unmet needs. Workers are employed in fieldwork, day care and residential settings and can possess a wide range of differing qualifications. Foster Carers, too, are increasingly caring for troubled children whose behaviour gives rise to confusion. Social Work, like other sectors of employment, is currently revising its current training arrangements. The Central Council for Education and Training in Social Work (CCETSW) has now introduced four frameworks for training all of which are integrated: Occupational Standards, Vocational Qualifications, Professional and Post-qualifying. The position of Directors of Social Work in Scotland is that Child Protection training should not be seen in isolation or grafted on to existing programmes, rather it should be located within the overall context of the established principles of good practice in relation to general child care. Similarly, Directors of Social Work in Scotland endorse the view put forward by CCETSW that any assessment of competence on the part of a worker should be based on observation of assessed practice rather than on academic achievement alone.

4.1.3 In addition to this, other occupational groups such as teachers, doctors, health workers and the police also require training on the subject of child protection. More will be said about this issue, and the issue of joint training, later.

4.2.0 CURRENT ARRANGEMENTS

4.2.1 The present position is that, across Scotland, there is a wide variation in the practice of individual local authorities. In-service training varies in relation to both its content and form. The bulk of this training is targeted at qualified field social workers whilst there are areas of need in other sectors, particularly in relation to residential care and Foster Carers. There is evidence to suggest, however, that attempts have been made to provide quality training opportunities making full use of innovative and imaginative techniques. Examples of this include:

- The expectation in some local authorities that workers will have undertaken between 5 and 10 days' training prior to being allocated child protection cases.

- The systematic use of the Open University Child Abuse and Neglect pack over a three year period for all staff working with under-fives in one Scottish local authority.
- A regular cycle of intensive joint police/social work courses.
- Training for senior managers in case conference skills.
- The use of coaching teams with a wide variety of experience and skills.

In addition to these in-service opportunities created by local authority training staff, two Scottish educational institutions have developed training courses which have academic validation: the University of Dundee and the Northern College.

4.2.2 The University of Dundee established a Diploma in Advanced Social Work (Child Protection) in 1989. This was part-funded by the Scottish Office in recognition of the fact that there was a need for post-qualifying training following the Cleveland Inquiry. A substantial proportion of the costs of training are incurred in the replacement of a small number of staff who have benefited from the opportunity to undertake post-qualifying training in child protection at the University of Dundee and have made a significant contribution to the work of their own agencies upon their return. The University offers courses at Certificate, Advanced Certificate, Diploma and Master levels. The Centre for Child Care and Protection Studies is also engaged in a number of research and other related activities. Directors of Social Work recognise the contribution that this course has made to social work practice in Scotland to date and looks forward to a full evaluation of the course by the University of York.

4.2.3 More recently, the Northern College in Dundee has also developed a formally assessed course in child protection work in conjunction with staff from Tayside Region Social Work Department. Students receive a certificate following successful completion of the course which is designed to reflect the changes in child protection work resulting from numerous inquiries and the growing body of research in child protection.

4.2.4 Whilst Directors value the contributions that have been made by academic institutions to date, basic training is essential and the quality can only be improved by local authorities with the aid of additional resources. The shortcomings in the present arrangements have been identified following national consultation undertaken to measure the present time and money being spent on training by all Regional and Island Authorities in Scotland. In some authorities there is little or no training provided, in others an attempt is made at providing systematic training opportunities.

4.3.0 OCCUPATIONAL AND VOCATIONAL TRAINING ARRANGEMENTS

4.3.1 Directors of Social Work believe that significant improvements in standards will emerge from exercises designed to define occupational standards and to link these with periods of in-service and College-based study. The involvement of employers in setting standards and defining the knowledge, attitudes and skills that specific groups of staff require to undertake particular tasks will ensure that, in the future, staff are competent to undertake the tasks expected of them. Directors believe that occupationally and vocationally trained staff will be in a position to make a significant contribution to the quality of life of both children and families receiving a service from the Social Work Department. We will also seek to ensure that issues in relation to child protection are set within the context of good practice in child care more generally.

4.4.0 QUALIFYING/PROFESSIONAL TRAINING

4.4.1 The Certificate of Qualification in Social Work (CQSW) is currently being replaced by the Diploma in Social Work. Both of these awards are made by the Central Council for Education and Training in Social Work. The CQSW was introduced in 1969 and it is the intention of CCETSW that all present CQSW courses will be replaced by the Diploma in Social Work courses by 1995. The Diploma will be more rigorously assessed in terms of the learning outcomes of particular students, and the quality of work undertaken by students on placement who will be assessed by accredited practice teachers. The role of the accredited practice teacher will be to work in partnership with academic staff to ensure that students are provided with learning opportunities which are of a high quality and are subject to rigorous assessment. The standards set by CCETSW will, however, only be met if Central Government decides that they merit appropriate resourcing.

4.4.2 The Diploma represents an attempt to ensure greater standardisation and seeks to lead qualifying social workers to a point where they are competent in appraising "the presence of risk indicators (of abuse, violence or exploitation) from analysis of social histories, from observation and from the advice and information of others" and can "assist in the assessment of individuals deemed at risk under Statute and demonstrate a working knowledge of the relevant legal and administrative procedures" (page 18, paragraph 2.4.1, Paper 30 from CCETSW).

4.4.3 Directors hold the view that newly qualified workers are not being adequately prepared to become involved in the complex processes of investigation, assessment and treatment of child abuse. We regret the failure of Central Government to accept the need for three year qualifying courses and would concur with Derek Saul, Chairman of CCETSW, that this decision was "inexplicable and disgraceful" (letter to Tony Newton, then Minister of Health on 30th June 1988). The Directors will continue to press for a three year qualifying course which will produce more skilled workers and bring us into line with social work training in Europe. We will also continue to argue for the resources in the interim to lead workers through both in-service and post-qualifying courses to a point where they are able to shoulder the formidable burdens that child protection work places upon them.

4.4.4 Directors welcome the proposal from CCETSW, funded by the Scottish Office, to seek to define the competencies involved in child protection work, whether it is carried out in field, day care or residential settings. This will help to clarify the knowledge, skills and attitudes that particular groups of staff require and will also assist in both the design of training programmes and the assessment of competence.

4.5.0 POST-QUALIFYING TRAINING

4.5.1 CCETSW has now developed a framework of post-qualifying education and training (A Framework for Continuing Professional Development, CCETSW, Paper 31) which seeks to ensure that workers will undertake post-qualifying studies up to the advanced award level in either social work practice, management research or training and education. It is expected that at post-qualifying level workers will have extended sufficiently the skills attained at qualifying level to enable them, for example, to be accountable for the liberty of people or to promote the empowerment of others. This is based on the assumption that at qualifying level social workers will be able to take responsibility for continuing their own learning and development. Directors of Social Work expect that CCETSW will make full use of CATS (Credit Accumulation and Transfer Schemes) when assessing workers at both post-qualifying and advanced award levels.

4.5.2 At an advanced level workers will receive recognition for their ability to provide leadership and expertise in their area of work. In so doing, workers will be able to gain recognition for the competencies that they acquire after qualification.

4.5.3 The need for post-qualifying and specialist training in child protection has been repeatedly reflected in the recommendations of reports from Public Inquiries into cases of child abuse and child sexual abuse. For example, in the report "A Child in Trust: the Report of the Panel of Inquiry into circumstances surrounding the death of Jasmine Beckford (1985)" the authors indicated that from the outset of their deliberations they became acutely aware that social work training needs to be enhanced, specifically to provide for specialist areas of work. Post-qualifying and advanced learning opportunities should be available to fieldworkers at front line and management levels and to staff working in day care and residential settings. Similarly, managers at more senior levels require to be assisted in taking on a range of tasks such as the chairing of case conferences, the process of consultation, the resolution of management disputes within and between organisations and in the management of public relations.

4.6.0 INTER-DISCIPLINARY TRAINING

4.6.1 Directors of Social Work recognise that there are presently a range of joint Police/Social Work initiatives operating within many local authorities in Scotland. This issue has recently been highlighted in a Scottish Office Report entitled "Child Sexual Abuse: The Professional Challenge to Social Work and Police". The Police are only one of a number of agencies involved in child protection work but they have a key role in the investigation of abuse and, consequently, joint training for social workers and police officers has an important part to play in locally agreed arrangements. This training should seek to develop staff with these responsibilities rather than limit itself to induction. Directors welcome the guidance on joint training contained in guidance issued in England and Wales by the Department of Health, "Working Together" (1991), and would welcome the same clear recommendations on training from the Scottish Office.

4.6.2 In addition to this very specialist area of work it has been noted that other agencies need to ensure that they too are providing their staff with appropriate training opportunities. At present much of the training is resourced by the staff of Social Work Departments. Other agencies must be actively encouraged to take it upon themselves to resource training for their own staff. One recent innovation in two local authorities has been to appoint inter-agency trainers who are responsible for organising inter-disciplinary training opportunities.

4.6.3 The introduction of the 1989 Children Act in England and Wales has created opportunities for training both in child care generally and in legislation for members of the judiciary. Similarly, people who carry the burden of making difficult and painful decisions about children and their families, such as Sheriffs and members of the Children's Panel, should be given the opportunity of undertaking training not only on legal matters, but on child care and child protection issues. This will ensure that they too are given every opportunity to reach decisions in a manner which is both informed and sensitive to the feelings and needs of all involved.

4.7.0 SUMMARY

4.7.1 The introduction of planned and resourced training strategies, involving the assessment of competence, observed practice and validation of learning, will lead to an improvement in the quality of social work practice with children and their families. It is recognised, however, that whilst training has a significant part to play in the improvement of practice we must also address wider issues, one of which is the failure to accept that child abuse is not solely an issue about dysfunctional families and aberrant adults, but is also very clearly related to structural inequalities within our society.

4.7.2 Directors challenge the wisdom of investing resources in costly judicial inquiries when those same resources could be used more profitably by investing in the development of staff through training. The announcement that the Scottish Office will provide a specific grant to support training for staff involved in residential child care and child protection is welcomed. The proposal that the Social Work Services Group will allocate the specific grant following consideration of plans put forward by local authorities is likely to give rise to a dialogue which is both positive and creative. In view of the recent restrictions placed on local government spending more generally, however, we hope that the Scottish Office will recognise that the grant from central government should be 100% of the total cost of training programmes, rather than the 70% which is currently proposed.

PART V

INTER-AGENCY COLLABORATION

5.1.0 WORKING TOGETHER – SHARED RESPONSIBILITIES

5.1.1 In Scotland, the protection of children is a responsibility shared with communities and discharged by a number of separate agencies: Health, Social Work, Police, Voluntary Organisations and the Children's Hearing System. These agencies work together within frameworks of law and government guidance. The nature and effectiveness of work undertaken at the interface between social work, the police and the child protection system is of critical significance to ensuring that the interests of children are protected and that any intervention made into family life is founded on their interests and tempered by a recognition and respect for the rights and responsibilities of parents.

5.1.2 Developing ways of recognising, understanding and responding to child abuse is an unfolding process. It involves an interplay between: public expectations and values; the growth, articulation and spread of knowledge; the willingness of the public, institutions, professional groups and agencies to face and absorb and act upon new ideas; the ability of agencies, institutions, professions and the legal processes designed to protect children's interests to adjust to change in a positive and proactive way. It is not only social work which must adjust and adapt its practice to the recognition of a scale of sexual abuse that was unthinkable before the mid-eighties.

5.1.3 Child abuse is difficult for the public to accept. Children are exposed to harmful, criminal, sexually exploitative and abusive acts. It is not uncommon for this to involve the carers of children. *Adults can and do organise themselves into conspiratorial networks to pursue the abuse of children and young people for sexual gratification and to avoid detection.* It presents demanding problems for professionals to come to terms with. Government guidance and the law cannot easily keep pace with it given the continuing growth of knowledge and the implication this has for practice. Establishing social work's contribution to the identification of adults who, acting alone or in collaboration with others to abuse children, will necessarily involve new learning and experience. Other agencies involved in the arrangements for child protection and the community at large will also have to adapt to and accommodate new knowledge.

5.1.4 Local authority Social Work Departments carry welfare as well as care and control responsibilities. Social workers are placed in an ever-shifting position between voluntary and compulsory intervention in relationships between parents and children. Changing knowledge leads social work to change its practice. Some changes are not always readily accepted by either professionals or the public. As a result, social workers have found themselves placed centre stage during the 1970s and 80s as British society and its institutions come to terms with child abuse. It is critically important that a sensitive and balanced legal and professional framework is established for dealing with the abuse of children.

5.1.5 Scotland's child protection system has been informed, if not influenced, in its development by events elsewhere in the United Kingdom. Government guidance has sought to distil knowledge and insights gained from a number of public inquiries into models of exce[illegible] which agencies, including those in Scotland, should strive to achieve. Such gui[illegible] sought to promote major changes in inter-agency relationships. None more [illegible] relationships between the Police and Social Work Departments. Boundaries and responsibilities have had to be re-negotiated and clarified in the face of new challenges. In particular, the traditional more clear-cut distinction between "welfare" and "criminal" in investigating and overcoming child abuse has become less clear.

5.1.6 Child protection practices are no longer based on ideas that children suffer abuse most predominantly because of the unaccountable and unpredictable acts of a few disturbed individuals who commit obvious physical and sexual assaults on them. As our understanding has grown, attention has necessarily focussed on the earlier recognition of both abuse and potential abuse. More appropriate ways of responding to children/victims and parents/perpetrators, actual or potential, have therefore had to be found. It is now accepted that, within the family, child abuse is not a discreet phenomenon unrelated to other difficulties or social problems. There is seen to be an interplay between the individual, the family and the community.

5.1.7 Child abuse in its various forms and degrees is not easily detected. Responding to it properly involves much more than the rescue of children and the conviction and punishment of adults. An effective, sensitive and positive approach to child abuse is now widely understood to require an inter-agency, multi-professional approach which ensures that a planned collection and evaluation of information takes place, and is used to respond sensitively and effectively to each particular situation, with the interests of the child being afforded the paramount consideration.

5.1.8 "Effective Intervention", published by the Scottish Office in 1989, summarises the implications of theoretical and organisational developments in the field of child abuse. It builds on previous government guidance and sets an agenda for future progress. In Scotland agencies have been brought together into "Area Review Committees". Under the leadership of Social Work Departments and informed by guidance, these agencies have formed loose federations charged with the responsibility to plan, monitor and evaluate child protection policies, practices and procedures, across and between agency boundaries. Increasingly practitioners from Health, Social Work, Police, Education and Voluntary Organisations now work together within jointly agreed inter and intra-agency frameworks which seek to co-ordinate their efforts and ensure coherent responses.

5.1.9 In a growing number of authorities there is regular liaison between practitioners who now jointly investigate abuse and meet regularly at planning meetings, and at child protection conferences, to consider the results of comprehensive assessments and to devise and review action plans. Currently greater emphasis is being placed on parental involvement in these processes. Considerable progress has been made in setting up these structures. Less progress has been made in agreeing the ethos and values necessary to work successfully within them, although much has been achieved in identifying the issues. Emphasis in guidance is now placed on ways to achieve better co-ordination through a clearer sense of purpose. Suggestions for achieving this include the refinement of joint policies, ...etter day-to-day working arrangements, providing more sensitised procedures ...ort systems and developing more joint training. The extent to which practitioners ...o work together, and, in cases of child sexual abuse, jointly interview children ...ate the information and risks, can vary widely across Scotland as in the rest of ...here is an urgent need to establish greater consistency of practice.

5.2.0 WORKING TOGETHER – THE POLICE AND SOCIAL WORK

5.2.1 In addition to the welfare duties under Part II of the Social Work (Scotland) Act 1968, Social Work Departments are obliged by Section 37, as amended by Section 83 of the Children Act 1975, to "cause inquiries" to be made when in receipt of information "suggesting" a child may be in need of compulsory measures of care. They are required to investigate and, where necessary, to pass information so collected to the Children's Panel. Amongst the grounds for such compulsory measures of care are crimes against children. The police, as the agency responsible in law for the investigation of crime, seek immediate referrals when suspicions of crime arise.

5.2.2 In referrals where there is a specific allegation of abuse amounting to prima facie evidence of assault against a child, referral to the police is likely to be clear cut. In circumstances where a child's behaviour gives rise to a suspicion that the child may have been sexually abused, the process of disquiet, suspicion, observing signs and indications, forming a professional judgement (all of which may fall well short of evidence that can be tested in court) can make the point of referral to the police difficult to determine.

5.2.3 The police have a duty to the welfare of the public which does not exclude children, as well as a duty to investigate crime. The basis of intervention in family life must rest not only on the establishment of primary criteria, such as an offence against the child, but also upon establishing that the child's parent or carer is unable to provide adequate care and appropriate levels of care and supervision of the child. For many police officers, the criteria used to test evidence in their day-to-day work is "beyond reasonable doubt" – a significantly different test of the "balance of probabilities" more usually applied in the context proceedings for compulsory measures of care involving children. In Scotland the separation of proceedings between the arrangements for proof and the care of the child can lead to a further blurring of criteria, with some Sheriffs construing the finding of offences committed against the child as effectively an allegation against the parents or carers requiring a higher standard of proof. The course of an investigation undertaken jointly rarely runs smoothly. It requires a framework for practice between the agencies, and a good measure of trust and respect between practitioners to be successful. Social workers would argue that the arrangements for the collection and collation of evidence must be subjugated to the interest of the child victims and meet the requirements of any proceedings in respect of the child, and should have a proper and appropriate involvement of parents/carers.

5.2.4 Perhaps understandably, given the evolving stage of practice between agencies, present guidance issued by government avoids giving definitive guidance on issues which might prove to be too controversial. Important decisions such as the nature of parental involvement in case conferences are left to individual agencies. The structures created and the lessons and values informing them are expected to provide the means for achieving an accommodation of viewpoint. Social work and the police in particular, are having to come to terms with very significant practical and philosophical problems arising from their different statutory responsibilities and customary methods of working. Achieving a participatory, sensitive and differential approach directed primarily at securing the welfare of children produces many dilemmas. Determining how to achieve, and on what basis, a proper balance between issues of welfare and crime in this endeavour is an unresolved issue between the police and social work in Scotland at this time.

5.2.5 Distinguishing between and choosing how to respond most appropriately to suspicions, allegations and disclosures of potential or actual abuse is a complex task. The police and social work are likely to see things differently. This is evidenced by the results of recent research (Child Sexual Abuse, The Professional Challenge to Social Work and Police, Scottish Office, 1990). Many of the issues raised by this research apply to the investigation of other forms of abuse. Current knowledge about abuse has sensitised agencies to warning signs and there is now an appreciation that abuse can present in a veiled way and be seen differently by different agencies. *Taking a child-centred inquiry through its various stages and keeping it as non-traumatic as possible for children and parents, whilst paying sufficient regard to the potential criminal dimension, can and does involve conflicts in approach and emphasis between the police and social work. These will not be solved to best effect either by routine undifferentiated joint action, or by unco-ordinated autonomous action.*

5.2.6 Decisions between the police and social work have to be made early based on some shared, agreed understandings and kept under constant review thereafter. Clearer statements of intent and prime objectives would assist in eliciting criteria on which to base such early and subsequent decision-making. More direct government guidance, given the different statutory responsibilities of the police and social work, would be helpful in engendering a clearer sense of common purpose.

5.2.7 Directors are concerned to ensure that the thrust of the 1970s and 80s towards resolute, urgent and proactive inter-agency investigations and interventions continues. This must not, however, be at the expense of creating a climate in which parents, children and young people feel unable to come forward for early assistance/treatment which will prevent or mitigate the likelihood of more serious abuse. The focus must remain on the child and his/her position within the family and community, and any action taken must be consistent with the welfare of the child/children concerned. Statements of prime objectives would enable focus to be maintained as inquiries, investigations, assessments and treatment plans unfold. The police and social work are moving closer together organisationally, if not ideologically, and further central guidance would facilitate and underpin quicker progress.

5.2.8 *Naivety or cynicism has no part in the investigation of child abuse but social workers do need a measure of scepticism. They understand that certain abusing parents can and do conceal, mislead and manipulate.* The police, on the other hand, are devising less interrogative approaches with the creation of specialist dedicated units to investigate crimes within families. They appreciate the need to broaden their vision away from the alleged act of abuse and to be sensitive to the child and family. There is now, therefore, much common ground between the two agencies and it is well-recognised that close co-ordination, liaison and communication need to take place between them. There are substantive as well as stylistic differences between the police and social work, and it is not always clear which agency and its predominant method of approach should take precedence in the interests of the child, the public or both. Flexible decision-making requires some commonly agreed criteria for resolving demarcation disputes. Alternatively, one agency, either the Procurator Fiscal or the Reporter acting in consultation with senior staff in police and social work, could be given authority to make the decisions when the emphasis for particular investigations cannot be fully agreed.

5.2.9 The detection of adults acting alone or in collaboration to abuse children for sexual gratification is a serious crime and a matter of great public concern. The involvement of children from more than one family by adults acting collaboratively to serve their own interests presents new and particular challenges to the agencies charged with responsibilities in this field. In investigation it would be expected that the police, because of their expertise and skill, will lead intelligence gathering operations and decide the most effective methods of gathering evidence, whether covert or overt. Given the difficulties of obtaining reliable forensic evidence from either physical examinations or from the statements of children who may have been pressed to silence, it anticipates very close co-operation taking place between the police, medical personnel and social work staff. Directors believe that the public would expect these examinations and interviews to be conducted in a manner consistent with the child's best interests and to be directed at gaining sufficient evidence to enable effective action to be taken for their future protection. Social Work Departments would be expected to treat the carers of children who are in their care, or in places of safety as a result of these inquiries, with respect and consideration. Genuine efforts must be made to keep parents/carers as fully informed about and involved with their children as possible. They should be kept advised on the progress of civil and criminal inquiries and proceedings, whilst avoiding undue distress to the children or risking the compromise of the effectiveness of these inquiries.

5.2.10 In such situations the Social Work Departments would act principally as advocates for the child's welfare in early strategy meetings with the police, Reporter and Procurator Fiscal, to ensure that the needs and rights of children and their parents are taken into account in any arrangements agreed. The interests of children require the detection and identification of people who may be acting in a collaborative way to abuse them. The planning and timing of any initial action will be critical to the process of collecting and collating the evidence. Circumstances are likely to be unique. The guiding principle should be that any action or process should have as its first consideration the interests of the child/victim. Actions designed to meet evidential requirements or needs should always be tested against that context. It has to be accepted that considerable demands will be placed on the agencies involved and their ability to meet such situations will be greatly influenced by the availability of resources and by the maturity achieved in their working relationships with the community, other professionals and agencies.

PART VI

SOCIAL WORK AND THE CHILDREN'S HEARING SYSTEM

6.1.0 THE LEGAL FRAMEWORK

6.1.1 The Directors of Social Work in Scotland strongly support the framework of Scottish Child Care Law and the Children's Hearing System. The legislative framework allows considerable scope for flexible application. A review of child care law in Scotland was completed by the Scottish Office in 1989 which substantially endorsed the existing arrangements, albeit with some significant modifications. The arguments put forward promoting change and revision of rules and procedures are made in the context of a strong commitment to the philosophy, principles and ethos which underlie both the law and the Children's Hearing System.

6.1.2 Parts II and III of the Social Work (Scotland) Act 1968 define the childcare responsibilities of Regional Councils. The Act requires the appointment of a Director of Social Work and the establishment of a Social Work Department. The provisions of Part III of the Act require the appointment of a Children's Panel Advisory Committee, the establishment of Children's Panels and the appointment of a Reporter. Practice in Social Work Departments and within the Children's Hearing System is shaped and influenced by government circulars and guidance and the application of Rules for Reporters and Children's Hearings.

6.1.3 The vision of the creators of the Children's Hearing System lay in the appreciation that successfully promoting the welfare of children goes beyond the control of behaviour, either theirs or that of their parents. Control and the use of authority, whilst required on occasions to protect welfare and develop potential, are unlikely to achieve real change in people. To be effective, controls need to be internalised. This process requires that people take responsibility for their actions and invest in a commitment to change. For this reason the Children's Hearing System operates in an informal inquisitorial mode seeking to involve children and parents and taking their views fully into account.

6.1.4 Chairpersons of Hearings have an important role and a measure of discretion in conducting business to minimise barriers to communication and encourage participation, whilst also enabling protection of children. Actively engaging parents, children and social workers in open, informal discussion is seen as the way to increase the chances of achieving a sound and broadly agreed foundation for moving forward.

6.1.5 The Children's Hearing seeks to enable a full dialogue among all parties prior to decisions. Disputes over the facts of referral, or situations in which parents or children/young people are aggrieved by decisions considered to be unreasonable, are resolved by reference to the Sheriff Court. If the child is not of an age to understand the facts or the grounds of referral, then there is an automatic referral to the Sheriff Court to prove the grounds of referral. These arrangements were designed to protect rights and ensure a sense of fairness about the proceedings.

6.1.6 The contribution required from social work is to offer professional advice in social background reports about the needs of children, and put forward views on how available services might be deployed to help them and their families. The Social Work Department provides a range of services likely to be required. The route to a Hearing is via the

Reporter who decides on the need for a Hearing: a decision which takes account not only of the facts that are presented as a basis for the referral, but also the apparent capacity of the child's parents/carers to provide adequate care and supervision. The Reporter progresses matters by calling Hearings and, where necessary, presenting evidence and representing their decisions to the Sheriff. The intention of the Act was to create a pluralistic, participatory system which sought to minimise damaging polarisation of views, whilst allowing the fullest expression of viewpoints and the testing of evidence when required. Roles were not tightly defined and operational procedures were kept to a minimum.

6.2.0 CURRENT PRACTICE

6.2.1 The interface between provision of services on a voluntary basis to promote a child's welfare and compulsory measures of care to protect welfare cannot be static. Perceptions and definitions of children's needs change as do society's perceptions of the rights and responsibilities of the state, parents and children. The Kilbrandon Committee (1964) anticipated that 95% of grounds in Hearing proceedings would be accepted by parents and children. Much of the language of Part III of the Act reflects the expectation that young people involved in delinquency and displaying troubled or troublesome behaviour would form the substantive part of the work of the Children's Hearings. Since the late 1970s, however, there has been a steady increase in care and protection cases. This is attributable to the expansion in knowledge and practice related to child abuse. A measure of the change that has taken place can be exampled by a perusal of a notable textbook – Children's Hearings; Martin & Murray; published by the Scottish Academic Press in 1976 – which gives a comprehensive account of the Children's Hearing System but makes little or no mention of non-accidental injury or child abuse.

6.2.2 The Social Work (Scotland) Act 1968 reflected the thinking of the mid sixties envisaging that "crimes" against children and cases of neglect would be more clear-cut than experience has shown to be the case. Concepts of child abuse in the form of non-accidental injury had yet to be widely accepted when the Act was passed. The different thresholds for child protection registration for civil and criminal proceedings, and the differential standards of proof between them, can make the area between voluntary and compulsory intervention difficult to negotiate and at times unpredictable. Reporters and Social Work Departments have, therefore, had to work closely together to clarify expectations and to communicate about specific children and their families.

6.2.3 Community-based services and multi-agency facilities have been developed to identify and respond to the needs of children and families. Although such service provision has grown, because of limitations on resources there has been a targeting of services towards children identified as being most vulnerable, and especially towards those assessed as being at risk of abuse, injury or neglect because of problems in the relationships between them and their parents.

6.2.4 Agencies providing services for children and families have been developing joint approaches particularly in Education, Health, the Voluntary Sector and Social Work Departments. This has led to the development of more flexible services capable of being delivered to families and children in their community. As such services grow so too do expectations, resulting in a keener awareness of the scarcity of such resources and the need to use them efficiently. Inevitably the response has been to develop a greater sense of prioritisation and targeting to those most in need. Practitioners have become aware of the need to plan more purposefully for children. Together these developments have resulted in earlier assessments and judgements about resource provision, linking these to plans consistent with the child care policies of Departments. *Such developments have had considerable implications for the operation of Children's Hearings and tend to underline their role in validating decisions taken about children and families, and testing and monitoring the care plans proposed.*

6.2.5 Increasingly, government guidance in child protection has given emphasis to collaborative inter-agency work in investigation and evaluation, highlighting the need for effective intervention and purposeful planning for children. This emphasis upon the skills, decision making and responsibilities of professionals can create a measure of tension when interfaced to a Panel system based on a philosophy of involving lay members in a process designed to promote open dialogue and achieve consensus and common-sense solutions. In serious cases of child abuse it is probable that either the nature of the problem or restriction of resources will limit options. In such cases it is unlikely that social workers will attend Hearings armed with a range of possible solutions, service options and choices for exploration. It is more likely they will arrive with clear plans and recommendations for the child's future care already worked out.

6.2.6 Some insights into the impact of these developments can be gleaned from research undertaken in 1988 (Study of Children's Hearings, Disposals in Relation to Resources). The research was prompted by the feeling of Panel members that local authorities were not paying sufficient regard to their responsibilities to give effect to Panel decisions. Far-reaching changes in resource deployment were seen to be constraining the availability of choice to Hearings. Some Panel members considered that child care policies were being developed which were out of step with the requirements of Hearings. The underlying concerns from Panel members about this changing role came through. The presentation by social workers of departmental views based on multi-disciplinary assessments, did effectively constrain decision-making. Hearings felt less able to influence recommendations of social workers who were seen as less persuadable participants in modern-day Hearings. Dissatisfaction, when it was expressed by Panel members, tended to centre on the actual day-to-day practices of social workers and their Departments. Some frustration was voiced by Panel members about their inability to have more direct influence on the day-to-day delivery of social work services. Although these views were not substantiated by the research, a high correlation between disposals made by Hearings and the recommendations put forward by Social Work Departments was demonstrated.

6.2.7 In most Regions the approach adopted to resolve difficulties is to maintain sound working relationships between Panels and Departments. Social Work Departments recognise the need for consultations when major changes in service delivery are being contemplated. These measures seek to establish dialogue and responsiveness to Panel members' expectations about overall services and the management of particular cases. Managers recognise that the commitment of social work staff and Panel members to major changes in policies or services is required if change is to prove effective.

6.3.0 DECISION MAKING FOR CHILDREN AND FAMILIES

6.3.1 Decisions about children are becoming more complex. A key principle in the creation of the Children's Hearing System is the sharing of responsibility for decisions and services between local authorities, parents, children and Panel members. An independent and impartial Panel will resolutely review the proposals and actions of Social Work Departments and consider these alongside the expressed views of parents and children before arriving at decisions.

6.3.2 Local authorities are increasingly open to consultation and to listening more effectively to service users. The introduction of Complaints Procedures, and in some authorities Children's Rights Officers, will hasten these developments. Parents are now more likely to be involved in case conferences, child care reviews and planning meetings, to consider options and service for the future. Considerable pre-Hearing work is, therefore, likely to take place.

6.3.3 The Hearing's role is to establish the basis of concern and test the reasonableness of proposals, arbitrating between existing disagreements, or examining and then refuting or confirming agreements. In cases of child protection a process of review and arbitration between differences is tending to replace the open-ended discussion and initiation of solutions and services, that the system originally envisaged. *The examination of the need for compulsory measures of care and what they ought to consist of, is likely today to involve Hearings adjudicating between representations being made to it, rather than a more open-minded search for common ground.* In care and protection cases the Hearings share with local authorities the responsibility for the protection, control, guidance or treatment of children at risk. Each will want to be satisfied that the care measures proposed will ensure the safety and well-being of the child concerned.

6.3.4 Given the complexity and gravity of child protection decisions, multi-agency and multi-disciplinary assessments must continue to inform the plans and recommendations being put to Children's Hearings. The development of overall child care policies and the integration of services around core values and objectives will also continue; so too will the prioritisation of service delivery. The participation of parents and children in pre-Hearing planning conferences and child protection case conferences will be further developed in the coming years. *The impartiality and independence of Hearings may require underpinning by measures designed to increase the opportunity for, and ability of, parents and children to participate in proceedings on a basis of greater equality.*

6.3.5 The process requires that the proposals and actions of social workers are critically tested. There is within the present arrangements provision for the use of safeguarders. The role of the safeguarder is to act as an independent assessor/adviser on behalf of the Hearing. Presently safeguarders are used in less than 1% of cases. In "care and protection cases" by definition there is often a conflict of interest between the parent and the child. It is, therefore, surprising that such limited use of this provision is presently being made. Whilst supporting the recommendations of the Child Care Law Review with regard to safeguarders, Directors would like to see further consideration being given to strengthening their role and availability, and more use made of their services in contentious cases. However, the role of the safeguarders is to act as an independent assessor/adviser on behalf of the Hearing and may not necessarily represent the interest of either child or parents.

6.3.6 The increasing complexity of child abuse cases during the late 1970s and 80s; the emergence of the children's rights movement; the role of the media in focusing the public accountability of social workers and Social Work Departments; the concerns of parents to secure representation of their interests; the problems faced by the Hearing System in maintaining independence and an inquisitorial mode of operation when cases before it involve major conflicts of interests; invite further and careful consideration of a number of key issues relating to the existing arrangements and responsibilities. These are:

- *the need for a greater clarification and definition of the role, authority and accountability of the Reporter in relation to the responsibilities and tasks of social workers and Social Work Departments in gathering information about referrals and making an initial evaluation of the risks to children and considering the steps necessary for their protection;*
- *to consider the need for further review and revision of the rules governing the conduct of Hearings and the rights of representation in the light of the growing complexity of cases, the balance to be struck between the paramountcy of the child's interests and the need to demonstrate respect for, and representation of, the rights of parents;*
- *in complex situations to hear and enable the interests of children and young people to be represented before a Children's Hearing independently of the interests of parents or the view of the Social Work Department;*
- *to consider parents' rights of access to legal aid and representation in respect of proceedings involving their children that carry risk to some rights of parents;*
- *the need to clarify in law parental rights of access to children in care and provide an appropriate mechanism of appeal when parents believe that access is being withheld or restricted unreasonably;*
- *the need to clarify in law the authority implicit in place of safety orders and warrants in respect of the medical examination of children in care.*

6.3.7 *Directors of Social Work believe that the rules and procedures which frame the work of Children's Hearings now require to be reviewed and revised. Revision should take account of the increased number of child abuse referrals, and the practice guidance which has been directed at Social Work Departments and other key agencies such as Health, Education and Police. These factors together with a shift in public attitudes require a more explicit balance to be demonstrated between the paramountcy of the interests of children and a respect for, and representation of, the interests of parents.*

6.4.0 SOCIAL WORK AND THE REPORTER

6.4.1 The Reporter occupies the pivotal position within the Children's Hearing System. The division of judicial and welfare functions in the Act separates the responsibilities of identifying and meeting the needs of children from demonstrating and proving the necessity for compulsory measures of care. The link provided by the Reporter between parents, referring agencies, service-providers, Panel members and the Sheriff Court is central to the operation of the Children's Hearing System.

6.4.2 It is the Reporter who frames the grounds of referral to a Children's Hearing. This acts as a welcome check and balance on the work of the Social Work Department. It is these facts which legitimise consideration being given to compulsory measures of care. The Reporter also considers the need for hearings on welfare grounds. Before these take place the possibility of using services voluntarily will have been considered. Where grounds evidencing the need for compulsory measures are not accepted by parents or children, these facts are put before a Sheriff by the Reporter and are subjected to the full rigours of an adversarial process. At Hearings the Reporter's role is limited to that of providing advice to Panel members on procedural and legal matters, though in practice Panel members do look to the Reporter for advice and guidance.

6.4.3 Where procedures or decisions of Hearings are seen as unreasonable by either parents or children they have a right of appeal to the Sheriff and it is the Reporter who represents the Hearing in these proceedings. Independence and impartiality are thus key attributes of the role both in the collection and presentation of facts and in addressing the welfare needs of children.

6.4.4 If it appears to the local authority that a child may be in need of such compulsory measures of care there is a statutory duty to refer the information to the Reporter. The Reporter, under the terms of Section 39, can decide to take no further action, and refer the case back if it is thought to be a proper course for the local authority to consider providing voluntary support. Where it appears to the Reporter that the child is in need of compulsory measures of care, steps will be taken to arrange a Children's Hearing having first been satisfied that the evidence is available for proof. If the grounds of the referral are challenged by a child or young person of an age of understanding or their parents, the evidence and the grounds upon which the proceedings are based are tested by due process in the Sheriff Court. Similarly, if the child is not of an age of understanding, the evidence is tested by due process in the Sheriff Court before the Panel considers any long term care plans for the child. The Act, therefore, leaves very wide room for discretion and allows and lends itself to different interpretations.

6.4.5 A high proportion of child protection cases occupy a grey area between the welfare responsibilities of Social Work Departments under Sections 12 and 15 of the 1968 Act and their mandatory duties under Sections 32 and 37 to formally involve Reporters to the Children's Panel. The legislation, in defining the relationship between Reporters and Social Work Departments, has allowed for considerable flexibility of approach. To some extent each Region applies and interprets the Act slightly differently according to local circumstances. Social Work Departments and Reporters necessarily work together as they are inter-dependent. Government oversees this process and influences it through guidance and formal and informal involvement. There are currently a number of different approaches being adopted but all seek to maintain an appropriate professional distance in working relationships, whilst allowing sufficient collaboration to ensure good decision-making. In cases where a referral is clear cut – an allegation is received and there is evidence of corroboration – the point of referral to the Reporter is rarely in dispute. If emergency powers are under consideration these will often be discussed, though it is important that any such discussion stops short of a direction from the Reporter unless his/her accountability for that direction is clarified.

6.4.6 How individual Reporters and Social Work Departments understand and agree to apply the provisions of the Act will be constrained by general developments throughout Scotland, but there is room for local choice and for local influences. Reporters can and do receive referrals from a variety of sources and will make inquiries and investigations of their own. The lead role assigned to Social Work Departments in relation to the child protection arrangements is, however, somewhat limited in this direction. Independent inquiries initiated by the Reporter still take place and Reporters can and do influence the course of inquiries and assessments undertaken by the different agencies involved. However, the primary responsibility rests with the Social Work Department which is increasingly held to public account for its professional actions in this field of work. Given the levels of public and professional concern, to both ensure effective intervention and protect people's rights, the interface between the responsibilities of the Reporter and the Social Work Department should be further defined.

6.4.7 *The extent to which Reporters exercise discretion in their role varies across Scotland. Likewise, the basis upon which they judge whether there is evidence to establish a prima facie basis for the consideration of compulsory measures of care may vary. Directors believe that it would be helpful to set the boundaries of the Reporter's discretion within an overall framework of arrangements introduced to ensure a sufficient measure of accountability to standardise practice.*

6.5.0 SOCIAL WORK AND THE CHILDREN'S PANEL

6.5.1 Increasing numbers and complexity of child abuse cases influence the interaction between agencies, between the Social Work Department and the Children's Panels, between Reporters and Panels, and issues related to social justice for parents and children arise and require to be addressed. Whilst functions remain separate, the balance of influence between the authorities has been affected by changes taking place in the organisation, management and delivery of social work services. This is particularly so in relation to the detailed guidance given to Social Work Departments by government in relation to child abuse. Hearings make decisions on the basis of reports before them including background reports from social workers, and discussions at Hearings between children, parents and social workers. Such reports will often reflect case conference discussion and multi-disciplinary/inter-agency evaluation. In these circumstances the Hearing's room for manoeuvre, and, therefore, the prospect of obtaining negotiated settlements and positively resolving disagreements, has become restricted. The intention of the system that discussions at Hearings would be the initiator of decisions, based on an exploration of information and the views of parents amd children/young people participating, can be difficult to achieve in such circumstances.

6.5.2 *Further consideration needs to be given to the ability of parents and children to represent their interests and participate on equal terms with local authorities when compulsory measures of care are being proposed.* The right of appeal of parents and children to the Sheriff Court is a right confined to the reasonableness of Hearings' decisions. Reports are only made fully available to parents and children at appeal stage when they are able to obtain legal aid to employ solicitors to represent their views. At present whilst the content of reports is usually shared with parents, they have no right to the reports as such. The Review of Child Care Law proposes changes which will require Reporters to notify children and parents of their right to see copies of reports, a right qualified by some exceptions. Directors support these proposals. When they disagree with the decisions of a Hearing the onus is placed on the child and parent to show these decisions have been unreasonably made. Where Sheriffs uphold appeal they remit cases back to the Panel for a reconsideration by them. Neither parents nor children have a right of legal representation during the Panel's initial decision-making or for that matter during any such reconsideration following the consideration of an appeal by the Sheriff Court. The arrangements provide for the provision of advice under the legal aid scheme and there is provision for parents to be supported and assisted by a friend. *Notwithstanding that the Hearing may decide on compulsory measures of care which may exclude or restrict both the parents' rights and access to the child, no provision is made for the formal representation of parents' interests.* Given that social workers may be presenting material on behalf of large and resourceful Departments with the endorsement of multi-disciplinary views, the position and interests of children and that of their parents may be seen to be unequally presented.

6.5.3 Recent debate about representing the interests of parents and children to participate more equally in the decision-making stages of Hearings tends to be framed in terms of whether or not they should be entitled to legal aid and legal representation at Hearings. The Child Care Law Review on considering this matter opposed such changes seeing them as introducing adversarial elements to Hearings.

6.5.4 *Effective intervention by the state in order to ensure certain minimum standards of care are guaranteed to children, and should be matched by the fullest possible opportunities being afforded to parents and children to challenge the definition of problems presented and the means for overcoming them. Hearings have the power to make momentous decisions about the future of children and families, this being legitimised by the proving of grounds and the right of appeal against decisions before the Sheriff Court. The right to intervene in a child's life, and come between the child and his/her parents by imposing compulsory measures of care is a powerful right. To be properly exercised it has to be based on a clear demonstration that the form of compulsion proposed is likely to further the welfare of the child, as well as linking any developmental problems with lack of care by the parent(s). More and more such questions of disposal are becoming questions of degree, and determining a proper response depends on the careful weighing of a number of factors.*

6.5.5 Many parents involved in "care and protection cases" will be from disadvantaged groups experiencing low income, unemployment, poor housing, lower levels of health and educational attainment. Self esteem, confidence and skills to represent their views cogently and coherently are likely to be impaired by these self same disadvantages. The ability to challenge views or present alternative proposals, or to know what alternatives there might be to those contained within social work reports (which whilst they may read they are not entitled to receive), is therefore likely to be low. Given the seriousness of the issues under consideration, conflict and disagreement are likely to be passionately held and pursued. Parents, children and young people need to feel and ensure that their views are represented. There is a need to find positive ways of enabling and encouraging parents and children to participate thoroughly in the examination of options presented to Hearings. Those parents who can afford solicitors are appointing them and asking them to attend as friend-advisers within the framework of the existing rules. This only compounds the disadvantages for those parents who do not have the financial means. *To command public confidence in complex cases involving compulsory measures of care it is essential that the Hearing System is regarded as being fair by parents and children. Some changes must therefore take place.*

6.5.6 One way forward may be to question whether it is reasonable to require that Children's Hearings can cope with the complete range of interventions in respect of children's interests; to consider whether the burden placed on lay Panel members in the most complex cases is a fair and reasonable one; to weigh the arguments for drawing a greater distinction in procedural terms between the needs of children and young people referred to the Hearing because they are in trouble, troubled or troublesome, and those who are referred because they are the victims of abusive behaviour and require an intervention from society to protect their health, welfare and development.

It is unlikely that the parents of children and young people coming before the Hearing on offence grounds will find themselves separated from their children on the first appearance, unless the offence has been particularly serious or the family circumstances are totally inadequate for the child's care. In relation to child abuse, compulsory measures of care may well be proposed at an initial hearing. The experience and expectations for parents and children will be strongly contrasted.

6.5.7 *In situations where the effect of the Hearing's decision is to deprive parents of their rights or children of their liberty, change should be introduced to allow the interests of children and parents to be separately represented. Given such serious considerations, Directors would argue that only experienced Panel members who have completed advanced training to a specified standard should be involved in dealing with abuse cases and cases potentially involving a loss of liberty for the child. The rules framing the Hearing itself should be amended to allow independent scrutiny of proposals by safeguarders in contentious cases where rights are in question, and separate representation of the interests of children and parents.*

6.6.0 REPRESENTATION OF CHILDREN AT HEARINGS

6.6.1 At present, children/young people cannot be heard by Children's Hearings outwith the presence of their parents unless the parents agree. It seems proper that children of an age to understand the process and/or express views should have a right of attendance but it also seems appropriate to allow them to be heard without the pressure of the situation or the presence of their parents inhibiting their contribution. This must be particularly so for young people of an age and ability to both understand the nature of the proceedings and express a view. Whilst the Chairperson of the Hearing has an existing discretion to determine the best way to achieve maximum participation by children in proceedings, the Panel members are restricted from hearing the views and opinions of children and young people unless they are expressed in the presence of their parents. In some circumstances it may be necessary to protect the immediate interests of the child by not requiring them to be present at the same time as parents. In cases where a parent is also an abuser the need to give space to children to express their views and feelings becomes more acute. The pain following the revelations of abuse with accompanying guilt, recriminations and conflict of loyalties, need more sensitive management and accommodation within the rules as they currently apply. Making a distinction between the abusing and non-abusing parent is important in this regard, as the non-abusing parent can be an important support to the child and can ally with professionals working to repair the damage and hurt caused by the abuse.

6.6.2 The Child Care Law Review, whilst aspiring to develop and extend the opportunities of children and families to participate in key decisions affecting their lives, has little to say about the arrangements for ensuring that the views and interests of children are properly and appropriately represented at Children's Hearings. Whilst the intention is to make a statutory prescription to give children and their parents rights to attend Child Care Reviews, there is little acknowledgement that parents and children may have interests that are different and may need assistance to participate at a hearing or a review on equal terms.

6.6.3 It is important that Hearings satisfy themselves that they have in place arrangements which will enable them to hear and take account of the views of children and young people. Children and young people should be encouraged to attend the Hearings and participate in proceedings, unless to do so can be clearly demonstrated to be against their best interests. Children and young people who have been the victims of abuse and ill-treatment should not be expected to repeat accounts of the abuse in the presence of the abusing person. *Directors of Social Work take the view that rules governing Hearings should be altered to allow the Chairperson of the Hearing to meet with the child or young person to hear their views and to agree with the child or young person how the content of their discussion is to be communicated to the other parties involved. In this context consideration should be given to the gender of the Chairperson.*

6.6.4 Children's interests in Children's Hearings may be better represented by a young person's advocate. Such a role might be developed by requiring each Children's Panel Advisory Committee to appoint a panel of people willing and suitably experienced to assist young people and children of an age to understand the proceedings with the expression of their views.

6.7.0 PARENTAL ACCESS TO CHILDREN SUBJECT TO COMPULSORY MEASURES OF CARE

6.7.1 Where a child is subject to a supervision requirement, access by parents or relatives is currently decided by the Hearing or by the local authority. Local authority practice is set out in a statutory code of practice issued by the Social Work Services Group in 1984.

6.7.2 Directors of Social Work support the changes proposed in the Child Care Law Review which underpin parents' rights of access and ensure that parents' views can be heard and considered in circumstances where the local authority is proposing to terminate or change access agreements previously agreed. The Review also proposes welcome clarification of the access arrangements to be attached to place of safety warrants where, in the absence of any specific conditions or an order preventing disclosure of the child's residence, a presumption of reasonable access is to be made. These proposed changes will be welcomed by practitioners and will clarify a significant omission in the present legal framework. Such issues add further weight to the additional steps that are required to ensure that parents not only have a right to be present, and a right to be advised, but also may require assistance to ensure their views and interests are represented at a Hearing. Equal consideration may require to be given to the interests and concerns of the children involved. There are mixed views as to whether the issues of disputed access should be first considered by a Hearing or stand referred to the Sheriff Court where representation of parents' and children's interests might be more readily secured.

6.7.3 When access has been terminated and such a decision or recommendation confirmed by a Children's Hearing, it is the view of Directors that parents should have a right of appeal to a Sheriff Court where their interests and that of the child can be formally represented.

6.8.0 EMERGENCY PROTECTION

6.8.1 Under the terms of Section 37 of the Social Work (Scotland) Act 1968, a constable or any person obtaining authority from a justice of the peace or a court may remove a child to a place of safety.

6.8.2 The condition for such action is that a reasonable belief is held that a crime against a child has been or is likely to be committed, i.e. there is immediate risk of harm. Situations of unnecessary suffering or serious impairment to health due to a lack of parental care are also covered. There is now widespread agreement that the law covering the immediate removal of children in such circumstances is deficient. Whilst it allows for decisive action, it is considered as leaving too much room for discretion and provides insufficient opportunities for parents or children to challenge both the initial and thereafter subsequent judgements and decisions. These problems are well discussed in available literature, (e.g. Children's Hearings and the Sheriff Court, B Kearney) and have been addressed by the Child Care Law Review.

6.8.3 Based on perceived past failures to protect children, Government guidance entitled "Effective Intervention" advises that investigations of suspicions and allegations of abuse must be undertaken speedily. In situations where it is believed children are in immediate danger, or where access to a child is refused and there are grounds for suspected abuse, agencies are advised to give urgent consideration to the need for a place of safety warrant.

6.8.4 Such action is reviewed by the Reporter at the earliest opportunity to consider the weight of evidence pointing to the need for a Children's Hearing and on this basis whether the child should remain apart from his/her family. Where a Reporter concludes that the evidence or circumstances cannot support the child's continued detention he/she has the right and responsibility to liberate the child. Thereafter events can take a number of different paths depending on the decisions and actions of the Reporter. Such orders can be used for a number of different purposes often depending on the strength of beliefs or suspicions and the availability of corroborating evidence. In situations of suspicion and uncertainty where parents refuse to co-operate they allow children to be removed whilst further inquiries are made. In circumstances which are more obviously dangerous and clear evidence exists, the warrant enables swift protective action with a speedy route to a Hearing. Whilst the Reporter's duty to consider the child's situation at the earliest possible opportunity provides a valuable early check on precipitative action, in practice there will often have been prior consultation between the Reporter and social workers. The discretion Reporters have to opt to either present grounds before a Hearing, or to simply advise on the circumstances under which warrants were taken, can be seen to disadvantage the rights of parents and children.

6.8.5 Currently there is no authority to undertake medical examinations, as opposed to observations, of children removed from their home on a warrant or place of safety order. Where a medical practitioner is satisfied that a young person is able to give informed consent, an examination may take place.

6.8.6 Medical examinations frequently fail to provide clear evidence, although they might confirm suspicions. Often statements from children are required as corroboration to meet the standards of proof necessary to protect them. There are also forms of sexual abuse unlikely to result in firm evidence, and interviews with children play a critical role. The timing of evaluative interviews with children, if they are to be effective and sensitive, have to be determined by the needs and circumstances of each individual child. The thorough investigation of sexual abuse allegations, whilst not always requiring the removal of children from their families, can prove to be extremely traumatic times for them and the suspected parent(s). Occasionally they are hazardous times for families. Any changes in the law should take these factors into account. Further flexibility might perhaps be introduced by allowing for extensions, and also by conferring on the Hearing the authority (after hearing from parents, children and social workers) to return children home under certain conditions deemed necessary to afford the fullest protection consistent with the child's welfare and with enabling further inquiries to be undertaken, i.e. the suspected perpetrator leaving the family home; the child remaining in the care of a non-abusing parent and/or the child attending a day nursery; a particular adult supervising the child at all times.

6.8.7 The awareness of the harm to the development potential of children through chronic long-standing but inconspicuous physical neglect, physical mistreatment, and emotional and sexual abuse, has led to the development of a number of assessment techniques for measuring the physical and emotional progress of children. Parental co-operation can be sought to allow such community-based assessments of the child's health or development and to examine more carefully the levels of care being offered. If parents agree, this then enables early consideration to be given to the type and degrees of supports and treatment that might be offered to families. On occasions, either because of an inability or an unwillingness to face up to the possibility of harm being caused to children, parents refuse to co-operate with agencies offering such assessments and services. Suspicions of such longer term cumulative harm may not justify the use of place of safety warrants and, without assessments providing evidence justifying intervention, compulsory measures of care cannot be sought.

6.8.8 It might be useful to give some consideration to the proper balance which should be struck in these circumstances between parental choice and the presence of concerns for the welfare of children. The need for some form of "child assessment order" within the framework of Scottish Child Care Law needs to be considered, particularly in view of the proposals to prescribe more precisely the use of place of safety warrants in the provisions for the emergency protection order.

6.8.9 Directors of Social Work support the recommendations of the Child Care Law Review in relation to emergency protection. If implemented as a whole they would significantly improve matters. Taken together they would discourage hasty intervention and provide greatly enhanced opportunities for parents and children to question the need for immediacy and to participate in the decision-making about subsequent warrants. By requiring evidence in support of grounds to put before parents and children at a Hearing within seven days, Reporters will need to be convinced that such evidence exists, or its existence can reasonably be expected to be established in that time. The authority of any order in relation to medical examinations and the involvement of the child in evaluative interviews would be clarified. The Hearing when called would be able to focus on the circumstances of the warrant and the immediate situation, and invite discussion on access arrangements and any further examinations and interviews. Parents and children would, therefore, have improved opportunities to put their views and to lodge appeals against the decision of a Hearing. It should be recognised that setting short timescales for the presentation of proof whilst generally welcomed, might compromise the future protection of some children unless provision is made for extension. There may be some very sound reasons, for example, for believing a child has been sexually abused, but further time may be required to elicit the supporting evidence or information.

PART VII

SOCIAL WORK IN ISLANDS AUTHORITIES AND SPARSELY POPULATED AREAS

7.1.1 Social Work to island communities in Scotland is provided by Strathclyde and Highland Regional Councils and the three Islands Authorities of Western Isles, Orkney and Shetland. Many of the issues and problems which they face in the field of child protection mirror the problems faced by mainland Authorities.

7.1.2 A clear distinction needs to be drawn between the resources provided to islands which are part of a larger mainland Authority and those which are solely Islands Authorities.

7.1.3 Island services which are part of a mainland service will find it easier to call upon additional resources when required, to draw on resources of staff familiar with the Authority's ethos and practice guidelines, and to exercise direct management control and authority over resources deployed.

7.1.4 Staff in Islands Authorities and other sparsely populated areas have from time to time to deal with child abuse cases, and these can be equally complex and just as difficult as cases in more populated areas. Factors pertaining to rurality and cultural differences will bring added features into consideration. Many of these factors will be positive, such as a strong sense of community promoting a sense of belonging and security. These same qualities can act to prevent a child speaking out where abuse has occurred.

7.1.5 Because such cases are not dealt with on a regular basis, it is even more important that training programmes are in place and are woven into the fabric of rural and islands Departments. It is also essential that overall policies and procedural guides are available to enhance practice.

7.1.6 Dissemination and assimilation of new professional knowledge is therefore equally essential for remoter rural areas, and Authorities should ensure that structures are in place for up-to-date continuing training and consultation in this field.

7.1.7 In unusual circumstances, assistance in the form of additional staff may be required by Islands Authorities from other agencies with little or no knowledge of island communities or culture. When outside help is necessary, basic ground rules should exist so that all parties know their responsibilities. Contingency plans should be drawn up by Islands Councils and Authorities with sparsely populated areas to accommodate such eventualities. Such plans should clarify the role of seconded staff, address issues of accountability and identify arrangements for support and supervision. A review of such plans should take place on a regular basis in order to cater for modification in light of new information.

7.1.8 While some Islands Authorities and sparsely populated areas lack specialist child care resources, such as Child Guidance Clinics or Family Centres, access can be arranged for specialist assistance to come to the area, or for the child(ren) and family to attend specialist resources in another area. All islands and rural areas seek to establish community foster parents and to make arrangements to support children and young people within their own community whenever possible.

In some areas foster parents are paid a retainer allowance for gaps in placements which can be lengthy, and efforts are being made to involve foster parents in training initiatives through the National Foster Care Association.

7.1.9 Continuity of language, culture, school and family contact underpins the efforts made to try to secure an adequate level of community based resources. If children are placed on the mainland, problems for them and their families are considerable, and involve among other things separation anxiety and lack of access, with children attributing even more blame to themselves, fuelled by distancing them from the home base. Added to these difficulties are those faced by professionals in monitoring and keeping a hold of the situation. It is, therefore, essential that Islands Authorities and rural areas tailor special arrangements for their particular situation which take account of the difficulties outlined.

7.1.10 The smallness and genericism of social work teams within island and sparsely populated rural communities present additional challenges to the effective management and supervision of complex cases. Whilst size is not necessarily a disadvantage, it does mean that staff need to think clearly and concisely about the roles they are fulfilling. In some isolated areas the main link for day to day supervision may be the telephone. Because of the isolation factor it is essential that case supervision on a planned regular face to face basis also takes place, so that social workers continue to respond to child protection cases from a base of social work values.

7.1.11 Confidentiality is an important concern in child protection cases. In Islands Authorities and rural areas it is inevitable that "professional" activity around a home is more likely to become public knowledge than a similar investigation in an urban setting. Experienced Social Work Managers have found that this need not hinder investigation, and staff should work on the assumption that all professionals involved will act in a professional way, unless there are extreme indicators to the contrary. Good inter-agency co-operation is essential in such settings and where it exists stress can be lessened. However, it is important that such inter-agency co-operation does not replace the social work supervision process, and that social workers in relative isolation manage to retain their social work identity in the face of the severe anxiety which work in the field of child protection can arouse in all disciplines.

7.1.12 Both the size of the Islands Authorities and the smallness of rural teams promote a reliance on informal verbal communication. It is important that all Islands and predominantly rural Authorities should have clear written procedures and that these are followed by staff irrespective of their location. These procedures will require monitoring and updating as in any mainland Authority.

7.1.13 There is a need for more focussed understanding of the problems of providing child protection services in Islands Authorities, island areas and sparsely populated areas.

7.1.14 In the field of child abuse as in many others, there is a tendency to think that islands and rural areas are somehow apart from the "mainstream" and are not likely to experience major social problems which the general public and remote administrators tend to associate with centres of population. An effective child protection service requires essentially the same mechanisms in an island area as it does in a city. However, the structures set up to make that service a reality will be different and may be costly.

7.1.15 Staff working in Islands Authorities feel that successive governments have failed to take account of the special problems faced by islands and remote areas in delivering a good standard of professional care services. Dealing with child abuse is an intensely personal service, and as such it is inevitably expensive to deliver. People living in islands and remote areas are entitled to as good a standard of service as those living in other communities, provided in a way that is suitable to the needs of the area.

7.1.16 Until Islands Authorities and less populated areas become the subjects of research in the field of service provision in the personal social services, and the findings made the subject of public debate, it will be difficult to argue for resources commensurate with the task, or to have any existing good practice publicised.

PART VIII

THE ROLE OF THE DIRECTOR AND SENIOR STAFF

8.1.1 Social Work Departments provide a wide range of personal care services to a wide range of people in need: children and families in trouble, at risk and in need; people who are elderly; people with physical handicaps, with learning difficulties (or mental handicaps), with mental health problems or those who have offended. Social Work services to children are critically significant both in terms of child protection and the special nature of responsibilities Departments have towards children who are formally in the care of the local authority. Pressures and demands on main grade social work staff are very high, both in terms of the volume of work and the intensity of the tasks staff are required to undertake.

8.1.2 Work in the field of child abuse is amongst the most stressful and demanding in social work practice. It is important that staff feel supported by managers, colleagues and their employers. The creation of a framework and ethos in which children's interests are protected; parents roles and responsibilities are respected; sound patterns of inter-agency work and multi-disciplinary collaboration are established; individual practitioners can bring their skill and experience to bear effectively, supported by their agency and the wider community; is a key responsibility of the Director of Social Work and senior managers.

8.1.3 The task of the Director and senior managers requires the exercise of professional leadership; the establishment of a framework of inter-agency co-operation; the preparation of practice guidance that takes account of government advice and new learning; the preparation and training of staff; the deployment of skilled and experienced personnel. Directors need to ensure the provision of a level of support and supervision of professional practice that gives staff adequate time to deal with the children and families involved together with the opportunity for structured objective appraisal of the issues, and the care plan it is proposed to adopt.

8.1.4 It is reasonable to expect that all authorities will have in place a mechanism for inter-agency - Health, Police, Social Work, Voluntary Organisations - co-ordination; guidelines to practice that are widely available to staff in all agencies and are regularly reviewed and up-dated; arrangements for maintaining established procedures for dealing with referrals, case conferences and case-recording. Most authorities have a training programme though, as highlighted, many authorities recognise that currently the levels of resource deployed in training are not adequate to meet either the needs of staff or the scale of the task. Main grade staff need a wider range of support services, foster-parents, residential homes, day centres and specialist skills to support their work and enable them to be effective.

8.1.5 Child abuse and child protection work has a high public profile. Media interest is consistent and often controversial, reflecting the ambivalence in public attitudes towards formal social work intervention in families or communities.

8.1.6 It is not the role of Directors of Social Work or their senior staff to act as case workers to particular children about whom the department has legitimate concern. In the normal course of events they should be able to rely upon the lines of accountability and structured supervision which exist within the organisation they head. Most Directors will have in place arrangements designed to alert them to situations which are out of the ordinary and have the potential to bring the distress of particular children and their families, together with the work of the social workers involved, into the glare of publicity. In such cases, Directors will seek to satisfy themselves that the presenting needs of the children and families concerned are being appropriately met. Anticipating media interest and coverage enables consideration to be given to the views the Department wants to express on the issues of public concern. All Departments will seek to avoid discussing the confidential details of individual families. Directors will need to judge when it is appropriate for them to deal with any media interest and when it is more appropriate for others to respond. A formal intervention in the lives of more than one family by more than one social worker requires preparation, response and resources that need careful management and co-ordination. All Directors would expect such a situation to be brought to their attention, and the extent to which they take direct control of the operational management will depend on circumstances, size of authority and the nature of the event. Such events occur rarely, they require established skill, experience and careful judgement to ensure that the interests of individual children and families are protected, staff supported and deployed effectively, and the interest of the authority and the confidence of the wider community are held in view.

8.1.7 Directors of Social Work are conscious of the accountability they are expected to carry for the service provided by their Departments. There are relatively few examples of other chief officials bearing responsibility and public accountability to the point where their position is no longer tenable. That is a challenge and risk borne by every Director of Social Work.

8.1.8 Social workers and Directors of Social Work operate within a framework of public accountability. Their responsibilities in child protection is a matter of continuing public concern, although little public attention is given to work undertaken successfully. Since the death of Maria Colwell numerous costly public inquiries have been conducted to examine the shortcomings of practice, in particular individual cases. Over the same period the government has, until quite recently, refused to invest more resources in social work training. Inquiries are in danger of becoming memorials to the children who die or the people who conduct them. There is little evidence to support the view that they are an effective vehicle for learning. Few, if any, professions develop skills, learning, practice, and organisational arrangements solely on the basis of unco-ordinated examination of cases or situations which have not been managed successfully. There is a need for more investment in effective research of successful practice. The knowledge base of the phenomena of child sexual abuse must be examined and developed in a disciplined and objective way and then disseminated effectively to competent practitioners. Inquiries, necessary as they sometimes are, must not be allowed to be a substitute for well thought out and structured appraisal of work undertaken in local authorities by a professional and credible inspectorate examining work in context of the scale of the need to be addressed and the resources available.

PART IX

SURVEY OF SCOTTISH CHILD PROTECTION REGISTERS 1990 – 1991

9.1.0 INTRODUCTION

Since the late 1970's all Social Work and Social Services Departments in Britain have developed special systems for managing cases of child protection. The general structure and approach of these systems have developed in response to central government guidance (Social Work Services Group, 1982; Scottish Office 1989; Department of Health, 1980, 1988, 1991), but many detailed aspects of the systems vary between local authorities. Surveys of these systems in Scotland and the statistics of their operation were undertaken in 1986 and in 1987 (ADSW, 1987, 1988). Part IX summarizes the findings of the latest survey covering the year July 1990 to June 1991.

In England and Wales, the National Society for the Prevention of Cruelty to Children (NSPCC) has since 1973 collected annual data on the registers that they manage on behalf of some local authorities (Creighton and Noyes, 1989). Annual returns have been collected centrally for England since 1988 (Department of Health, 1989). Both the NSPCC and the Department of Health reports are restricted to register statistics, but the Department of Health is currently funding a study that is providing details of English register systems and the factors associated with variations in registration rates (Gibbons, 1991).

In Scotland the Scottish Office Social Work Services Group (SWSG) is currently developing a national system for child abuse management information, which should provide annual central statistics on the management of child protection cases in Scotland.

9.2.0 REFERRAL OF CASES

Child protection systems can only respond to cases that are brought to their attention and so all social work departments have procedural guidelines for investigating any referrals that are made to them. If initial investigations of a referral reveal concerns about the welfare of a child then an inter disciplinary case conference may be convened. This case conference has the power to place the child's name upon the local child protection register. Registration invokes other aspects of the procedures and these guide further work with the case including the drawing up of a child protection plan and regular review case conferences.

9.2.1 Investigations

Social work has a statutory responsibility to investigate and respond to child abuse and so investigations will be recorded in some way by the department (such as in case files). Eight regions in Scotland were able to provide statistics on investigations (see table 9.2.3 and Appendix 1), but only four regions use formal recording systems.

Formal recording system: Central, Grampian, Strathclyde, Tayside.

In Shetland referrals that are considered to have been malicious are recorded separately.

9.2.2. Case Strategy Discussions

Case conferences (cc's) are the main forum for inter-agency discussion and planning for child abuse and child protection. In the past case discussions were often discouraged because they might lead to the avoidance of the formal case conference system. Some regions have always used case discussions for the less serious cases where child abuse procedures are not thought to be necessary. With the growth of sexual abuse and other complex cases government guidance for Scotland now refers to the possible use of pre-planning or strategy meetings (SWSG, 1989, para 3.21). Guidance for England states that early strategy discussions are essential (Department of Health, 1991, para 5.13.1). The main argument for introducing a pre case conference forum for discussion is to ensure good inter agency planning and cooperation during the initial investigation, particularly between police and social work who both have important but different statutory responsiblities. There are, however, other reasons why these pre-conference discussions have become attractive.

One reason is the increasing emphasis on involving parents in case conferences (Scottish Office, 1989, para 4.19; Department of Health, 1991, para 6.5). In the initial stages of investigating complex or sensitive cases the agencies may wish to confer before informing the parents of their concerns. If parents are to be invited to the initial case conference there may be a preference for an early strategy discussion and a slightly postponed initial case conference.

A second and related attraction of strategy discussions is the reticence of some agencies about the consequences of referring all but the most clear cut cases to social work. Case discussions or strategy meetings allow workers from other agencies to raise their concerns without necessarily triggering a full scale investigation.

a) No formal case strategy discussion system
Five regions state that they do not formally use stategy case discussions, though some discussion may occur between professionals before a case conference is called. This is probably increasing now that many regions have arrangements with the Police for joint investigation of special cases which imply pre case conference discussions.

No formal system: Fife, Grampian, Highland, Orkney, Shetland.

b) Less serious cases
Two regions state that they use case discussions for cases which will probably not require a formal case conference: Fife and Shetland.

c) Complex cases
Seven regions stated that they use case discussions for particularly sensitive or difficult cases:

Sexual abuse: Borders*, Lothian, Strathclyde, Tayside (* *under consideration and used by some teams*).

Joint Police/SW investigations: Central, Western Isles.

Complex cases: Dumfries & Galloway.

Lothian Region also has pre-planning meetings for any case (not just child protection) where the professionals feel that a meeting to pool and discuss information would be useful.

9.2.3 Initial Case Conferences

If the initial investigation suggests that there is a basis for concern then an initial case conference is called to pool information and to determine what next steps should be taken.

Appendix 1 details the percentage of investigations that result in an initial case conference as well as the proportion of these conferences that result in registration. Table 9.2.3 contrasts the relative rates and percentages for different regions.

TABLE 9.2.3

Relative Rates of Investigation, Conferencing and Registration

Region	*Rate of Investigations*	*Chance that Investigation will be Conferenced*	*Chance that Conference will register case*
Borders	–	–	Medium
Central	High	Very Low	Medium
Dumfries	–	–	Medium
Fife	–	–	–
Grampian	High	Medium	Low
Highland	–	–	–
Lothian	Medium	Medium	High
Orkney	Medium	High	Low
Shetland	Very Low	Medium	High
Strathclyde	High	Low	Medium
Tayside	Very High	Low	Low
Western Isles	Very Low	High	High
SCOTLAND	High	Medium	Medium

The table suggests that regions fall into the following five broad categories. The average figures for the whole of Scotland fall somewhere between categories (i) and (ii).

(i) High rate of investigation but then less likely to register: Central, Grampian, Strathclyde, Tayside.

(ii) Medium rate of investigation with high chance of being conferenced, but then only a medium chance of being registered: Orkney.

(iii) Medium rate of investigation with quite high chance of registration: Lothian.

(iv) Low rate of investigation but then quite high chance of registration: Shetland, Western Isles.

9.3.0 REGISTRATION RATES FOR SCOTLAND

Children are placed upon and removed from child protection registers by inter disciplinary case conferences. The main exceptions are de-registrations without a conference when children are transferred to the register of another region, have become adult, or have died.

The number of children placed on registers is sometimes portrayed as an estimate of the extent of child abuse in the population. However, it is increasingly recognized that there are also many other factors that determine register size.

9.3.1 Factors Influencing Statistics

a) Identification: extent that cases are brought to the attention of social work. The extent that children, parents, wider family and community, and non social work agencies and staff are able to identify children at risk and are willing to refer this information to the relevant agencies.

b) Policy and practice re child protection: formal and informal policies determining the extent that cases known to agencies are referred to social work and whether these then progress to case conference and registration.

c) Turnover: the length of time registered cases remain on the register. Removing children's names from the register after only a short period of registration will tend to reduce the overall size of the register (and vice versa).

The effect of turnover of cases on registration rates has largely been ignored in the literature but it is easily calculated and has been included in this and previous Scottish survey reports. In the absence of data on turnover, the rates of new registrations per year provide a clearer view of cases being registered than the total registration rate.

9.3.2 Scottish Totals

Since 1987 the total registration rate for Scotland has risen by a third despite the 1991 figures showing (a) a slight increase in turnover of cases and (b) a rate of new registrations similar to that of 1987 and below the overall registration rate for 1991. The conclusion must be that the increase in register size occured between 1988 and 1990.

TABLE 9.3.2

Scottish Rates and Turnover 1987-1991

	1987	*1990*	*1991*
Registration rate	2.58	3.55	3.43
Rate of new registrations	2.01	–	2.56
Turnover	71%	–	84%

see Appendix 2 for detailed figures

Over the year 1990-1991 the Scottish registration rate has fallen slightly. Turnover of cases has also fallen, which suggests that fewer cases are being introduced into the system. This is confirmed by the rate of new registrations being less than the overall registration rate. If this continues, the total Scottish registration rate is likely to return to 1987 levels.

9.4.0 REGIONAL REGISTRATION RATES 1987-1991

Most regions have increased their rate of new registrations of cases since 1987. The increased registrations are associated with increases in the overall register size but this is modified by changes in turnover. Tayside's turnover has increased markedly with the register size remaining nearly the same.

TABLE 9.4.0

Changes in Regional Rates 1987-1991

Region	*New Registrations*	*Turnover*	*Register*	*1991 Size*
Borders	Up × 2	Down × 0.25	Up × 2.3	Medium
Central	Up × 1.7	Down × 0.21	Up × 2.1	Medium
Dumfries	Up × 1.8	Up × 0.03	Up × 1.75	High
Fife	Down × 0.3	Down × 0.17	Down × 0.25	Very Low
Grampian	Up × 3.3	Up × 0.42	Up × 2.3	Medium
Highlands	Up × 2.2	Up × 0.32	Up × 1.8	High
Lothian	Up × 1.3	Down × 0.02	Up × 1.4	High
Orkney	Zero in 1987	+82% from zero	Down × 0.1	Medium
Shetland	Zero in 1987	+31% from zero	Up × 15.4	Medium
Strathclyde	Up × 1.25	Down × 0.11	Up × 1.4	Medium
Tayside	Up × 1.3	Up × 0.70	Down × 0.05	Medium
Western Isles	Up × 3.6	+33% from zero	Up × 1.3	Medium

See Appendix 2 for detailed figures

9.5.0 REGIONAL REGISTRATION RATES 1990-1991

9.5.1 Size of 1991 Registers

The registration rates of most regions range from 2 to 4 children per thousand population. Three regions have larger registers and one has a much smaller register:

Large: Dumfries, Highland, Lothian.

Medium: Borders, Central, Grampian, Orkney, Shetland, Strathclyde, Tayside, Western Isles.

Small: Fife.

9.5.2 Change in Size of Register Over Year

Most regions remained within 15% of their previous size over the year. Three regions grew more than 15% and one region fell by more than 15%.

Change < 15%: Borders, Central, Dumfries, Fife, Highland, Shetland, Strathclyde.
Increase > 15%: Grampian, Lothian, Orkney, Western Isles.
Decrease > 15%: Tayside.

9.5.3 Turnover

In general, a high registration rate with a low turnover would result in a register increasing in size, whilst a low registration rate with a high turnover would result in a register decreasing in size. This is not fully evident in the table because of the form of the summary data.

TABLE 9.5.3

Regional Variations in Register Size and Turnover

Region	*Rate of New Registrations*	*Turnover*	*Register Size in 1991*	*Change in Size 1990-91*
Borders	Low	Medium	Medium	Same
Central	Medium	Medium	Medium	Same
Dumfries	High	Medium	High	Same
Fife	Very Low	Medium	Very Low	Same
Grampian	Medium	Medium	Medium	Up
Highland	High	High	High	Same
Lothian	Medium	Low	High	Up
Orkney	Medium	Medium	Medium	Up
Shetland	Low	Very Low	Medium	Same
Strathclyde	Medium	Medium	Medium	Same
Tayside	Medium	Medium	Medium	Down
Western Isles	Low	Very Low	Medium	Up

A clearer view of the changes over the year is given by constrasting rates of new registration with both turnover and the size of the 1990 register. This results in four different types of change in the regional registers:

a) Rate of new registrations approximately equal to registration rate at one time therefore most cases must turnover during the year. Confirmed by high turnover rate: Borders, Central, Dumfries & Galloway, Fife, Highland, Strathclyde, Tayside.

b) As (a), but lower turnover rate leads to growth in register over year: Grampian, Orkney.

c) Low rate of new registrations compared to register size with low turnover rate leading to growth in register over year: Lothian, Western Isles.

d) Very low rate of new registrations compared to register size, so no growth in register size despite low turnover rate: Shetland.

9.6.0 TYPES OF ABUSE

The types of abuse or risk of abuse associated with children being placed upon child abuse registers is meant to be evident from the register categories in which they are placed. The picture is confused by the use of at risk categories which confound the area of concern (i.e. abuse) and the nature or type of that concern (e.g. level or type of risk or level or type of knowledge that abuse has occurred). This section considers the types of abuse that it is possible to ascertain from register data. Section 9.7.0 considers the range of register categories in operation in Scotland.

9.6.1 Scottish Totals

Since 1987 the proportion of physical abuse cases and emotional abuse cases has remained constant, the proportion of sexual abuse cases has risen by 30%, and the proportion of neglect cases has risen by two thirds. Several regions have stopped using general risk categories (see section 9.7.2). The regions which continue to use general risk categories also continue to use them for a third of their cases. The overall increase in sexual abuse and neglect cases may be due to the discontinuation of general risk categories in other regions.

TABLE 9.6.1

Types of Abuse 1987-1991

Abuse	*1987*	*1990*	*1991*
Physical	32%	32%	31%
Sexual	15%	18%	23%
Emotional	9%	9.5%	10%
Neglect	12%	21%	22%
Failure to Thrive	–	1.2%	0.5%
Unspecified Risk	35%	37%*	34%*

** relates to only 4 or 5 regions and accounts for total percentages exceeding 100%.*

9.6.2 Regional Figures 1987-1991

Appendix 3 presents the changes in proportions of different register categories between 1987 and 1991. The changes in proportions of different types of abuse are obscured by the changes in register categories over this time (see section 9.7.2).

The proportion of sexual abuse cases increased in three regions but they all discontinued important risk categories:

– Grampian discontinued a category for siblings which contained 43% of 1987 cases.

– Lothian discontinued an at risk category which contained 20% of 1987 cases.

– Tayside discontinued a small at risk category and three sexual abuse mix categories.

Three regions introduced emotional abuse as a category and the number of cases so registered varied from zero to 14%.

Grampian and Fife introduced the category of neglect. In 1991 Fife had 12% neglect cases and previously had not distinguished cases into categories. In 1991 Grampian had 16% neglect cases, but had discontinued a category for siblings that contained 43% of the 1987 register. Dumfries and Galloway had a neglect category in 1987 and this increased by 32% by 1991, but the region had discontinued a general risk category which accounted for 50% of the 1987 register.

Failure to thrive is a little used category and there were few changes in the number of cases so registered.

9.6.3 Regional Figures 1990-1991

Appendix 4 presents detailed figures for the numbers and proportions of cases placed on different register categories in each region in 1990 and 1991. The variation between regions in the use of risk categories on the register obscures any variation there may be between regions in the proportions of different types of abuse cases. Changes over the year in proportions of different types of abuse are relatively small considering the small numbers of cases in each category in each region.

9.7.0 REGISTER CATEGORIES

The types of child abuse are derived from the categories within which children are placed on the register. Central guidance for Scotland (Scottish Office, 1989, para 2.6) recommended six categories of Physical Injury, Physical Neglect, Failure to Thrive (FTT), Sexual Abuse, Emotional Abuse, and Children At Risk. The guidance acknowledged that there was variation across Scotland in the categories used and suggested that this may change with the planned implementation of a national child protection management information system. The categories currently in use are fully shown in Appendices 3 and 4.

9.7.1 Categories of Abuse/Area of Concern

Most categories of registration refer to a particular type of abuse that is of concern to the case conference registering the child. At risk categories are different and are considered under Section 9.7.2.

The abuse categories in operation can be listed according to the 1989 SWSG guidance:

SWSG list: Borders, Central, Dumfries, Tayside.
SWSG list plus Adopted Children, Dead Children: Lothian.
SWSG list plus Poisoning, Deprived of Special Care, Other/Unspecified: Highland.
SWSG list minus Emotional Abuse, Neglect, FTT: Orkney*, Western Isles. * *changes planned*
SWSG list minus FTT but plus Other/Unspecified: Grampian.
SWSG list minus Emotional Abuse: Fife, Strathclyde.
No categories: Shetland.

Grampian and Highland Regions both allow registration of some cases into an unspecified category when the other categories are not appropriate. Lothian and Dumfries have some unclassified cases where the category of registration is not known. This can occur where a region changes the categories on a register and already registered cases are not re-classified.

Two regions allow cases to be coded into a first and second category of abuse: Fife, Tayside.

9.7.2 Risk Categories/Nature of Concern

The report of the last Scottish survey (ADSW, 1988) examined the way that At Risk categories are different to abuse categories. At Risk categories refer to the nature of the professional concern (in this case risk) rather than the area of abuse that there is concern about (e.g. sexual abuse). The report suggested that at risk categories were offering a second criteria of registration and that there would be logic in separating this from the abuse register categories. Recently guidance for England has discontinued the risk category of Grave Concern (Department of Health, 1991).

Four regions do not use at risk categories, four have at risk categories similar to the abuse categories, and four regions have developed an alternative to at risk categories.

a) No classification of risk/nature of concern

Three regions make no use of separate at risk categories or of a separate variable for rating level of concern: Borders, Grampian, Shetland.

Borders did use an at risk category in 1987, Grampian and Shetland did not.

b) Standard at risk categories

Five regions have at risk categories similar to standard abuse categories. Two of these regions have more than one at risk category and these are the same categories that they used in 1987. The two other regions did not differentiate registrations into any categories in 1987. They have now introduced a category system and have adopted the standard categories including one of at risk.

1 at risk category: Fife, Orkney, Western Isles.

2 at risk categories (Physical and Sexual): Strathclyde.

4 at risk categories (Injury, Neglect, Sexual, and Referred into Region): Highland.

c) Separate nature of concern variables

Four regions have developed the policy advocated in the 1987 survey report of discontinuing the At Risk category and replacing it with a separate variable indicating nature or level of concern. These levels of concern can be associated with any of the different categories of abuse (area of concern).

The classification of nature of concern developed by Dumfries, Central, and Tayside regions consider (i) the level of certainty that abuse has occurred, and (ii) whether there is risk even if there is not suspicion that abuse has occurred. The system developed by Lothian also specifies particular types of risk.

– 3 levels of concern (Actual, Suspicion, At Risk): Dumfries.

– 4 levels of concern (Certain/Proven, Very Suspicious, Suspicious, At Risk): Central, Tayside.

– 7 levels/types of concern (4 levels above plus Abuse to Other Children in Household, Presence of Abuser of Other Children, Mix of these two): Lothian.

Two regions classify further aspects of the nature of the concerns involved in registered cases. Lothian's registration form has a list of 23 factors important to the decision to register. Tayside lists 16 possible 'state of child' categories plus a 'concern only' category used for risks arising from the presence of a Schedule 1 Offender.

9.8.0 CRITERIA FOR REGISTRATION

Classifying the nature of concern that led to registration also bears upon the criteria for registration as the presence of certain criteria can become the means of categorizing cases placed upon the register.

Many regions publish procedures that provide broad outlines of the criteria for registration. Procedures also, to varying degrees, consider the appropriateness of specific circumstances for registration.

9.8.1 Register Siblings

Most regions would not automatically register siblings, registration would depend upon the risks in particular cases. The table shows that, in practice, an average of more than one child per family is registered. As some children come from single child families, there must be many multiple registrations in other families. Evidence for this is shown in Borders and Grampian, whose 1987 registers had specific categories for siblings making up 43% and 34% respectively of all cases. It is likely that siblings now make up a significant proportion of children placed on general at risk categories. These issues can become clearer with the use of separate nature of concern variables that can code whether the child is in the same household or subject to the same risks as another registered child.

TABLE 9.8.1

Number of children registered per family

Region	*Number*
Borders	1.67
Central	1.78
Dumfries	1.84
Fife*	1.64
Grampian	1.77
Highland	no data
Lothian	1.71
Orkney	no data
Shetland	2
Strathclyde	2.25
Tayside*	1.7
Western Isles	2

*All data based on new registrations except for * where based on registrations at June 1991.*

9.8.2 Register Children who have Died?

No region registers children who have died (though Lothian retains names of children who die in suspicious circumstances whilst on the register).

9.8.3 Register Unborn Children?

Three regions allow the registration of unborn children and a further three regions have systems for including unborn children into their child protection systems.

a) Register unborn children: Borders, Grampian, Western Isles.

b) Do not register, but a case conference can decide for registration to be actioned automatically at birth: Dumfries, Central.

c) Do not register, but unborn child can be put on alert section of register (system of temporary alert to register during investigations) until birth: Strathclyde.

d) Do not register: Central, Fife, Highland, Lothian, Orkney, Shetland, Tayside.

9.8.4 Organized/Multiple Abuse

Most regions do not have special categories or formal arrangements for these type of cases. Central would invoke a pre case conference planning meeting. Both Central and Strathclyde would invoke joint police/social work procedures. Other regions might in practice also adopt these responses.

9.8.5 Abuse Occurring in Institutions

Some regions (Central, Fife, Grampian, Highland, Tayside) state they they would register these cases, but in practice the child would be likely to be removed from the source of the alleged risk.

9.9.0 REMOVING CHILDREN FROM THE REGISTER

The turnover of cases on the register depends upon the basis on which children's names are removed from the register.

9.9.1 De-register Children Received into Care?

The following policies and practice occur:

a) Basic policy and practice is to de-register children although obvious exceptions of temporary receptions into care and where there is access involving a suspected perpetrator: Central, Fife, Borders.

b) No policy to de-register but this may occur dependent on the circumstances (e.g. level of access, supervision of access, plans for permanent alternative care): Dumfries, Grampian, Highland, Lothian, Orkney, Shetland, Strathclyde, Tayside.

c) Lothian region maintains the addresses of some children on the register after they have been adopted into new families if there are concerns about any children remaining in the household. In essence this is a means of registering a household rather than a child. These cases are placed under a separate register category and are reviewed internally on an annual basis rather than being subject to the normal six monthly inter-agency case conference review system. Lothian uses the same system for cases where a registered child dies in very suspicious circumstances (see 9.9.2). Other regions do not have these options, although they could register remaining children as being at risk.

9.9.2 Remove Dead Children from Register?

All regions except Lothian remove children from the register if they die. Lothian keeps children on the register if it is believed that they may have died from abuse and that the remaining children in the household might be at risk. The same system is used for some adopted children (see 9.9.1.c).

9.9.3 Categories of De-registration

Only two regions classify the reasons for removing a child's name from the register. A further region (Dumfries & Galloway) lists factors to be taken into account for de-registration, and these factors are similar to the categories used by Lothian and Tayside.

Lothian

Aged 16 years	7%
Original concerns discredited	15%
Improved child care environment	59%
Child in long term care/adopted	10%
Child with other stable carers	3%
Transferred to other authority	2%
Reasons not clear	3%

Tayside no figures yet available

Aged > 16 years
Improved home situation
No improvement, but no evidence of continued risk
Child with other permanent carers
Transfer to other authority/family move out of area
Child dead

9.10.0 PERPETRATORS OF ABUSE

It has been argued that perpetrators of abuse should be registered in addition or instead of children. This seemingly attractive idea raises complex issues of civil liberties and so lists of perpetrators are usually restricted to cases where the facts have been established in court.

9.10.1 Suspected Perpetrators in Registered Cases

Only Highland and Lothian Regions formally record perpetrators (other than Schedule I Offenders). In Highland this includes cases where there is strong professional belief that an individual has abused children. In Lothian it includes adults who have admitted to the abuse. Other regions (for example, Strathclyde and Tayside) may identify suspected perpetrators on proformas of investigation or registration.

9.10.2 Schedule I Offenders

The prison service informs social work departments of the release of these offenders into their regions. Sometimes this is simply informing the department that a prisoner who is about to be released has stated that he will be going to an address within the region. In other cases the social work department is requested to provide a report for an application for a release on licence. The adequacy of the operation of these systems is one subject of discussion of a working party on Schedule I Offenders at the Social Work Services Group.

The system of notification raises two main questions for this survey:

a) Relationship to child protection procedures
On being informed of the imminent release of an offender most departments would investigate the household to assess whether: the household is already known to the department, whether children are present, whether the children are likely to be at risk, and whether their carers are aware of these risks.

The relationship of this system to arrangements for child protection varies as follows:

– small department and so in practice similar staff responsible for offenders and for child protection: Orkney*, Shetland. *(* but plans for specialized staff).*

– the officers responsible for child protection are automatically informed and therefore potentially involved in all cases notified to the department: Central, Lothian, Strathclyde.

– the Prison Service notifies the officer responsible for offender issues who liaises directly with local teams. Officers responsible for child protection only become involved if there are concerns about risks to children and child protection procedures are invoked: Borders, Dumfries, Fife, Grampian*, Highland, Tayside, Western Isles. *(* but would usually involve child care and little distinction between this and child protection).*

b) Registers of Schedule I Offenders

Most regions retain the names of all offenders notified to them. There is therefore the potential for creating a register of these offenders. Four regions (Central, Grampian, Highland, Tayside) place the offenders' names upon their computerized client information systems. Although the computer systems are primarily for case management purposes, they can begin to approximate to a register of perpetrators. The systems can create lists of offenders by name, address, and a range of other variables. The systems can also be interrogated to determine whether a particular individual is or is not known as an offender. Once an offender is placed on one of these computer systems there is no obvious focus (such as a case conference) for their name to be removed.

9.11.0 MANAGEMENT OF CASE CONFERENCES

9.11.1 Chairing of Conferences

Conferences are normally convened and chaired by social work departments. The only exception in Scotland is Shetland where the Chief Area Medical Officer acts as chair.

There are two important issues concerning the choice of officer to chair conferences. The first is the relative seniority of the officer. As the terms used to describe different grades vary across regions it is simpler to describe seniority by the number of management steps from the case worker to conference chair.

The second important issue is whether the chair person has line management responsibility for the case being considered. The table shows that in seven regions the chair does have line responsiblity.

TABLE 9.11.1

Seniority and Line Management of Case Conference Chair

Region	*Management Steps*	*Case Manager?*	*Designation*
Borders	1	no	Senior S.W. (child protection)
Central	2/3	no*	P.O. or A.P.O. child protection (**but binding decision making powers*)
Dumfries	2	yes	Principal S.W. for child protection
review cc:	1	yes	Senior S.W. managing case
Fife	2/3	yes	Area Organiser or Depute Area Organiser
since 1/10/91:	1	no	Team Manager
Grampian *either:*	2/3	yes	Divisional Officer or Area Manager
or:	1	no	Senior S.W. trained in child protection
Highland	2	yes	Principal Officer
Lothian	1/2	yes	Area Officer or Senior S.W.
West Lothian:	1	no	Senior S.W. not involved in case
Orkney	2	yes	Assistant Director Fieldwork
Shetland	n.a.	no	Chief Area Medical Officer
Strathclyde	2	yes	Area Manager
Tayside	2/3	yes	Different levels of service manager
Western Isles	2/3	yes	Assistant Director or Area Manager

S.W.: Social Worker   P.O.: Principal Officer   A.P.O.: Assistant Principal Officer

9.11.2 Professional Attendance at Case Conferences

Lothian is one of the few regions to collect data on professional attendance at case conferences. The table below describes the numbers of regions reporting different professional groups attending case conferences. The data is only impressionistic but indicates which disciplines other than social work are thought to routinely attend case conferences. These findings are similar to those reported for Glasgow in the mid 1980's (Gough *et al*, 1987) and routine data from Lothian, except that Lothian achieves a relatively better attendance from General Practitioners.

TABLE 9.11.2

Number of Regions Indicating Attendance of Different Professionals

Profession	*All/Most CCS*	*Initial CCs*	*Occasional CCs*
Health Visitor	11	–	1
Senior Nursing Officer	8	–	–
School H.V. or Nurse	1	–	1
General Practitioner	4	–	2
Clinical Med. Officer	3	–	2
Hospital doctor	–	2	2
Psychiatrist	–	–	2
Psychologist	2	–	1
Teacher	11	–	1
Nursery staff	5	–	1
Police	9	2	–
Reporter	4	2	1
Procurator Fiscal	2	–	1
Police Surgeon	–	2	–
RSSPCC/Vol. Orgs.	1	–	–
Foster Parent	–	–	1

9.11.3 Parental Attendance at Case Conferences

Central guidance emphasizes the need to involve parents in decision making (Scottish Office, 1989) and most social work departments are in favour in principle of involving parents in case conferences. There can, however, be ambivalence about parental attendance arising from (a) the discussion of fact finding material (one of the attractions of strategy meetings), and (b) the concerns of other agencies, such as medical staff, about the presence of parents.

Practice concerning parental attendance varies considerably between cases and within and between regions, but the general situation is summarized by the following:

All conferences: Borders, Fife.
All except fact finding part of initial conference: Lothian, Strathclyde.
All except initial conference: Central, Western Isles.
Part of most conferences: Grampian, Highland, Orkney, Shetland, Tayside.
Conference recommending de-registration + some review cc's: Dumfries & Galloway.

9.12.0 REGISTER SYSTEMS AND MANAGEMENT INFORMATION

9.12.1 Use of Computers

Six regions have placed their child protection registers on computer systems. For three regions these are stand alone systems. For the three others the register is integrated into the wider client information system. Other regions, for example Grampian, may happen to have registered children on a client information system but not in a form for managing the register.

a) Register not on computer: Borders, Grampian, Highland, Orkney, Shetland, Western Isles.

b) On stand alone computer system: Dumfries, Lothian, Strathclyde.

c) On computer as part of wider client information system: Central*, Fife, Tayside.

(also have manual card index stand alone system).*

9.12.2 Active or Passive System

Computer systems can be used as a more sophisticated version of a passive manual system, but it can also be used in a more active form to help manage individual cases. For example, indicating when a review conference is due.

– System updated with changes within a case but not used to manage cases: Dumfries, Fife.

– System actively manages cases: Central, Lothian, Tayside, Strathclyde *(since summer 1991).*

9.12.3 Checks to Register

In all regions the agencies presented at the Area Review Committees are entitled to check if a child whom they are concerned about is on the regional register. Regions vary in the number of enquiries they receive, the breadth of the search that they undertake, and the consequences of any check.

a) Number of checks

Several regions do not record that a check has been made. In Tayside there is no means to record this information as field staff and selected medical staff have direct access to some levels of the computerized client information system. Medical staff, for example, can only access whether a name is on the child protection register.

Several regions do note whether a check has been made, but do not collate the figures. In Dumfries*, Shetland and Western Isles very few checks are made *(* local teams used to use monthly computer printouts of registrations in their area, but dangers from lists not being up to date nor being region wide).*

Data on checks to the register is only available for three regions:

TABLE 9.12.3

Source and Outcome of Checks to Register

Region	*Own SW*	*Other SW*	*RSSPCC*	*Police*	*Health*	*Other*	*Total*
Grampian	48 (43+ve)	3 (0+ve)	–	–	–	1 (0+ve)	52 (3+ve)
Highland	63	–	1	2	–	–	66
Strathclyde	1522	–	–	–	46	–	1568 (380+ve)

b) Breadth of check

Regions vary in the breadth of the search made for a check. Only three regions restrict this to the current register.

Current register only: Dumfries, Grampian, Lothian.

Current and previous registrations: Borders*, Highland. *(*up to 2 years old).*

Current and previous registrations, alerts, and investigations: Strathclyde.
Wider client system: Central, Fife, Shetland*, Tayside. (*would also enquire of other agencies).*

Checks very infrequent, cases all very well known to local staff: Orkney, Western Isles.

c) Consequences of check
In most regions it is up to the inquirer to follow through the concerns that led to the check. Some regions would ask the reasons for the concern (for example, Shetland), some would inform the local team manager (for example, Borders and Highland), others would follow up cases where a number of enquiries were made about one child or family. This is, of course, only possible in regions that record that a check has been made.

9.13.0 SPECIALIST POSTS

Regions vary in the extent that child protection is differentiated from other child care work and organisational systems. Little data was collected by the survey on this issue but the following categories summarize the general situation for the Scottish regions:

a) No specialist posts with child protection being an integral part of child care: Grampian, Highland, Orkney*, Shetland, Western Isles. (*plans for specialist posts).

b) No specialist teams, but some child protection specific officers: Borders, Lothian*, Strathclyde, Tayside. (*plans for specialist workers).

c) Child protection practitioners/specialists or investigation teams: Central, Dumfries (many unfilled posts), West Fife, Dundee East, Tayside Special Unit (Polepark).

9.14.0 REFERENCES

Association of Directors of Social Work, 'Scottish Child Abuse Statistics 1985-1986'. Internal report prepared by D.A. Gough, July 1987.

Association of Directors of Social Work, 'Scottish Child Abuse Statistics 1987', Report prepared for ADSW and Social Services Research Group by D.A. Gough, June 1988.

Creighton, S.J., and Noyes, P. 'Child Abuse Trends in England and Wales 1983-87', National Society for the Prevention of Cruelty to Children, London, 1989.

Department of Health, 'Working Together: A guide to inter-agency co-operation for the protection of children from abuse', HMSO, 1988.

Department of Health, 'Working Together. Under the Children Act 1989: A guide to arrangements for inter-agency co-operation for the protection of children from abuse', HMSO, 1991.

Department of Health, 'Survey of Children and Young Persons on Child Protection Registers Year Ending 31 March 1988 in England', HMSO, 1989.

Department of Health and Social Security, 'Child Abuse: Central Register Systems', LASSL (80)20, 1980.

Gibbons, J., 'Operation of Child Protection Registers. Interim report of postal survey'. Unpublished report, University of East Anglia, August 1991.

Gough, D.A., Boddy, F.A., Dunning, N., and Stone, F.H. 'A Longitudinal Study of Child Abuse in Glasgow', Report to Scottish Office, 1987.

Scottish Office, 'Effective Intervention. Child Abuse: Guidance on co-operation in Scotland', HMSO, 1989.

Social Work Services Group, 'Child Abuse', SW4/82, Scottish Office, 1982.

APPENDIX I

RATE OF INVESTIGATIONS AND PROPORTIONS CONFERENCED AND REGISTERED

	** Investigations*	*Case Discussions*	*% of Investigations Conferenced*	*% of Conferences Registered*
BORDERS		0.89		67%
CENTRAL	13.33		22%	67%
DUMFRIES				64%
FIFE				
GRAMPIAN	11.01		56%	50%
HIGHLAND				
LOTHIAN	5.78		63%	85%
ORKNEY	5.45		95%	57%
SHETLAND	1.51		62.5%	80%
STRATHCLYDE	15.46		37%	48%
TAYSIDE	17.48		36%	54%
WESTERN ISLES	2.15	2.15	86%	83%
WEIGHTED AVERAGE	13.2		43%	57%

** Rates per thousand children under 16 years.*

APPENDIX II

CHANGES IN SIZE OF REGISTERS, RATE OF NEW REGISTRATIONS, AND TURNOVER 1990/91

	Child Population	*Registration Rate 1/7/90*	*Registration Rate 30/6/91*	*Change in Rate 1990-91*	*Rate of New Registrations*	*Turnover*	*Change in Rate of New Registrations 1987-1991*	*Change in Total Registration Rate 1987-1991*
BORDERS	19,047	2.42	2.21	91%	1.84	85%	202%	227%
CENTRAL	54,914	3.3	3.59	109%	3.04	83%	172%	215%
DUMFRIES	28,582	5.7	5.7	100%	4.37	77%	180%	175%
FIFE	70,749	0.6	0.7	112%	0.6	82%	64%	74%
GRAMPIAN*	102,469	1.7	2.39	141%	2.02	78%	331%	234%
HIGHLAND**	43,427	6.15	5.94	97%	6.17	102%	224%	179%
LOTHIAN	138,076	4.64	5.58	120%	3.09	51%	130%	141%
ORKNEY	4,034	2.73	3.47	127%	2.97	82%	WAS ZERO	90%
SHETLAND	5,284	2.46	2.46	100%	0.76	31%	WAS ZERO	1,537%
STRATHCLYDE	474,030	3.57	3.09	87%	2.85	93%	125%	140%
TAYSIDE	75,850	5.02	3.65	73%	3.39	97%	132%	94%
WESTERN ISLES**	6,522	2.30	3.07	133%	1.53	33%	356%	135%
TOTALS	1,022,984	3.55	3.43		2.56	84%	127%	133%

Child Population rates are per thousand children under 16 years.
Turnover is the number of de-registrations as a percentage of 1990 register.
** data is for 3/90-3/91 ** data is for 8/90-8/91*

APPENDIX III

CHANGES IN REGISTER CATEGORIES AS A PROPORTION OF REGISTERED TOTALS 1987 – 1991

Region		*Totals*	*Physical*	*Sexual*	*Emotional*	*Neglect*	*FTT*	*At Risk*	*At Risk Injury*	*At Risk Neglect*	*Suspected Alleged Sexual*	*Deprived Special Care/ Treatment*	*Poisoning or Suspected*	*At Risk Referred In*	*Other/ Unspecified*	*Not Classified*	*Adopted*	*Dead*
Borders					Old (0%)	Old (0%)		Old (14%)								Old * (Sibling 43%)		
Central			−8%	−2%	New 14%	−2%	New 1%											
Dumfries			+17%	+1%	New 3%	+32%	+1%	Old (50%)								Old* (Susp. Abuse 0%)		
Fife			New 31%	New 12%		New 12%	New 2%	New 43%										
Grampian			−1%	+17%	New 5%	New 16%									−1%	Old* (Sibling 34%)		
Highland			−6%	−3%	Same	+6%	+0.3%		−11%	−5%	+13%	−1%	Same	−0.7%	−9%	Same		
Lothian			+18%	+13%	+2%	+3%	−1%	Old (−20%)								New 4%	−0.7%	−0.4%
Orkney			New 17%	New 14%				New 14%										
Shetland			NO CATEGORIES															
Strathclyde			−7%	−2%		+12%	−0.9%	−12%			+10%							
Tayside			−4%	+9%	−4%	+28%	−1%	Old (−5%)		Old (−2%)	Old* (CSA Mix 5%)				Old* (Phys+Neg 1%)	Old* (Phys+Emo 16%)		
Western Isles			New 10%	New 10%				New 80%										

New: a new category not used in this Region in 1987. Old: a category no longer used (1987 % in brackets). Old*: name (and 1987 % in brackets) of other discontinued categories.

APPENDIX IV

CATEGORIES ON REGISTER 1990/91 RAW FIGURES + PERCENTAGE OF REGISTER

Region	Date	Totals	Physical	Sexual	Emotional	Neglect	FTT	At Risk	At Risk Injury	At Risk Neglect	Suspected Alleged Sexual	Deprived Special Care/ Treatment	Poisoning or Suspected	At Risk Referred In	Other/ Unspecified	Not Classified	Adopted	Dead
Borders	7/90 6/91	46 42	CATEGORY SYSTEM RE-INTRODUCED APRIL 1991															
Central	7/90 6/91	181 197	90 50% 81 41%	41 23% 46 23%	4 2% 27 14%	44 24% 41 21%	2 1% 2 1%											
Dumfries	7/90 6/91	163 163	77 47% 65 40%	24 15% 18 11%	0 0% 5 3%	54 33% 72 44%	2 1% 2 1%									6 4% 1 0.6%		
Fife	7/90 6/91	45 51	16 36% 16 31%	4 9% 6 12%		1 2% 6 12%	1 2% 1 2%	23 51% 22 43%										
Grampian	3/90 3/91	174 245	87 50% 93 38%	43 25% 72 29%	4 2% 13 5%	32 18% 40 16%									8 5% 27 11%			
Highland	3/90 3/91	267 258	41 15% 43 17%	14 5% 9 3%	0 0% 3 1%	18 7% 28 11%	3 1% 1 0.3%		56 21% 67 26%	21 8% 8 3%	64 24% 62 24%	0 0% 0 0%	1 0.4% 0 0%	5 2% 1 0.3%	25 9% 36 14%	19 7% 0 0%		
Lothian	7/90 5/91	641 770	239 39% 293 38%	116 18% 160 21%	115 18% 138 18%	126 20% 134 17%	9 1.4% 10 1%									28 4% 28 4%	3 0.5% 2 0.3%	5 0.8% 5 0.6%
Orkney	6/91	11 14	DATA NOT AVAILABLE, BUT AT LEAST 8 CASES SEXUAL ABUSE – REMAINDER, IF ANY, PHYSICAL ABUSE. 10 71%	2 14%				2 14%										
Shetland	7/90 6/91	13 13	No Categories															
Strathclyde	7/90 6/91	1691 1463	394 23% 297 20%	114 7% 118 8%		301 18% 306 21%	19 1% 2 0.1%	694 41% 507 35%			169 10% 233 16%							
Tayside	7/90 6/91	381 277	144 38% 90 32%	55 14% 67 24%	45 12% 17 6%	132 35% 103 37%	5 1% 0 0%											
Western Isles	8/90 8/91	15 20	0 0% 2 10%	4 27% 2 10%				11 73% 16 80%										

BIBLIOGRAPHY

BAIN O, and SAUNDERS M (1990); "Out in the Open"; Virago Press

BELL, L (1991); "Preliminary Report on Child Abuse Procedures"; University of Dundee

BIRCHALL, E (1990); "The Frequency of Child Abuse" - in Child Abuse, Public Policy and Professional Practice; Ed - Olive Stevenson

BLOM-COOPER, L (1985); "A Child in Trust"; The Report of the Inquiry into the Death of Jasmine Beckford; London Borough of Brent

BRITISH PSYCHOLOGICAL SOCIETY (1990); "Psychologists and Child Sexual Abuse"; British Psychology Society, Leicester

BUTLER-SLOSS, E (1988); "Report of the Inquiry into Child Abuse in Cleveland 1987"; HMSO: London

CAMPBELL, B (1988); "Unofficial Secrets"; Virago, London

CHILDREN ACT, 1975

CLARK, A (1987); "Women's Silence, Men's Violence - Sexual Assault in England 1770 - 1845"; Pandora, London

DALE, P (1986); "Dangerous Families"; Tavistock Publications

DEPARTMENT OF HEALTH AND SOCIAL SECURITY (1980); "Child Abuse"; Central Register Systems LASSL (80) 4; HMSO London

DHSS 1986 DRAFT; Child Abuse, Working Together

DINGWALL, R (1990); "Predicting Child Abuse and Neglect", in Child Abuse - Public Policy and Professional Practice; Ed - Olive Stevenson, Wheatsheaf

DOH 1988; "Protecting Children"; A guide for social workers undertaking a comprehensive assessment

FALLER, K (1988); "Child Sexual Abuse"; An interdisciplinary manual

FINKELHOR, D et al (1986); "A Source Book on Child Sexual Abuse"; Sage: London

FINKELHOR, D et al (1988); "Nursery Crimes"; Sexual abuse in day care; Sage: London

FOX HARDING, L (1991); "Perspectives in Child Care Policy"; Longman

GIOVANNONI and BECCERRA (1979); "Defining Child Abuse"; N Y Free Press

GLASGOW, D (1989); Play-based investigative assessment of children who may have been sexually abused. Chapter 9 in Wattam C et al (ed) "Child Sexual Abuse, Listening, Hearing and Validating the Experiences of Children"; Longman: Essex

GORDON, L (1988); "Heroes in their Own Lives : The Politics and History of Family Violence"; Virago, London

GOUGH, D (1988); "Child Abuse Statistics 1987"; ADSW

HALL, L and LLOYD, S (1989); "Surviving Child Sexual Abuse"; Falmer Press

HALLETT, C (1986); in "Parental Participation in Case Conferences"; BASPCAN

HAUGAARD and REPUCCI (1988) ; "Child Sexual Abuse"

HOLLOWS, A (1991); "Investigating Sex Abuse. Are We Playing It Too Safe?"; Community Care 27/6/91 Inside: (i) - (ii)

JONES, D and McQUISTON, J (1986); "Interviewing the Sexually Abused Child"; Gaskell: London

JONES, D P H (1991); "Ritualism and Child Sexual Abuse"; Child Abuse and Neglect Vol. 15 pp 163 - 170

KALISCH, B J (1978); "Child Abuse and Neglect - An Annotated Bibliography"; Westport Press

KELLY, L et al (1991); "Research Report on Frequency of Unwanted Sexual Interaction in Young People Under 18 Years"; Child Abuse Studies Unit: Ladbroke House, London

KEMPE, H (1962); "The Battered Child Syndrome" in Journal of Americal Medical Association 181: 17-22

KOLVIN, I, et al (1988); "Child Sexual Abuse": Principles of Good Practice; Brit. J. Hospital Medicine; Jan. p54 - 62

MacFARLANE, K and WATERMAN, J (eds) (1986); "Sexual Abuse of Young Children" Holt Rinehart & Winston

McLEOD, M and SAVAGE, E (1988); "Challenging the Orthodoxy in Family Secrets" Feminist Review, special issue

MORRISON, J et al (1987); "Twenty Myths that Justify not Tackling Child Sexual Abuse"; Social Work Today, July 20 p9 - 11

NELSON, S (1986); "Incest: Fact and Myth"; Stramullion: Edinburgh

O'HARA, M (1991); "Children on Film"; Community Care 27.6.91 Inside pp (ii) - (iii)

PACKMAN, J and JORDAN, B (1991); "The Children Act - Looking Forward, Looking Back" in British Journal of Social Work, Vol 21, No 4

PARTON, N (1985); "The Politics of Child Abuse"; MacMillan

PIGOT, T et al (1989); "Report of the Advisory Group on Video Evidence"; Home Office: London

ROBERTS, J et al (1987); "A Sample of Sexually Abused Children in Scotland"; The Child and Family Trust Ltd, Glasgow

ROBERTS, J et al (1991); "Report on Research into Child Sexual Abuse"; Child and Family Trust Ltd, Glasgow

ROBERTS, J, DEMPSTER, H, TAYLOR, C and McMILLAN, B (1991); "A Study of the Frequency of Child Sexual Abuse in One Scottish Region"; Child Abuse Review, Vol 5 No. 1 pp 3 - 6

SALTER, A (1988); "Treating Child Sex Offenders and Their Victims"; Sage: London

S.E.D. (1990); "Protection of Children From Abuse. The Role of Education Authorities, Schools and Teachers"; Circular 10 22/5/90

SGROI, S (1982); "Handbook of Clinical Intervention in Child Sexual Abuse"; D C Heath: Lexington

SOCIAL WORK (SCOTLAND) ACT, 1968

SSI (1990); Inspection of "Child Protection Cases in Rochdale"; DOH

STEVENSON, O (1989); "Multi-disciplinary Work in Child Protection"; Ch. 8 in Stevenson O (ed). Child Abuse. Public Policy and Professional Practice; Harvester, Wheatsheaf: London

SUMMIT, R (1983); "The Child Sexual Abuse Accommodation Syndrome". Child Abuse and Neglect; Vol. 7 p177 - 193

SWSG (1989); "Effective Intervention"; Guidance on Co-operation in Scotland; HMSO: Edinburgh

WILD, N J and WYNNE, J (1986); "Child Sex Rings" in British Medical Journal Vol 293, 183-185

WILL, D (1989); "Feminism, Child Sexual Abuse and the Long Overdue Demise of Systems Mysticism" in Association for Family Therapy Newsletter, Spring 1989, 12-15

WYATT, G and PETERS, S (1986); "Methodological Considerations in Research on the Prevalence of Child Sexual Abuse" in Child Abuse and Neglect Vol 10, 241-251

WYATT, G (1988); "Lasting Effects of Child Sexual Abuse"; Sage, Beverly Hills

WYRE, R (1990); "Working with Sex Abuse". In Working with the Sex Offender; Issues for Policy and Training; Home Office and Department of Health, March 1990